HOW TO MARKET YOURSELF . . . YOURSELF!

How to Market Yourself . . .

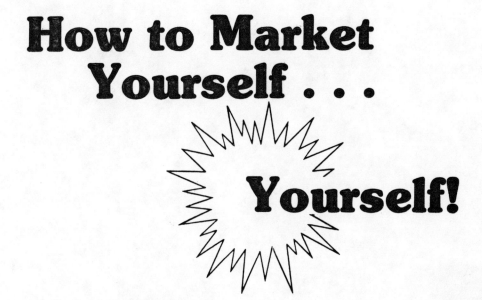

Yourself!

The Executive Job Changing Guide Book

BRUCE E. MOSES

PRO-SEARCH, INC.   Olympia Fields, Illinois

Published by PRO-SEARCH, INC.
3612 West 211th Street
Olympia Fields, Illinois 60461

Library of Congress Catalog No. 79–63505
ISBN 0-9602540-0-5

Printed in the United States of America

First Edition

For
Karen, Michael, Amy, and Heather

CONTENTS

INTRODUCTION

As the title implies, this book was written to serve as a tool for any executive or professional who is contemplating a job change. I will guide the individual from the moment he decides he wants to change jobs, to the acceptance of that new outstanding offer. I will begin by trying to serve as a catalyst in helping him decide if he even should change jobs, or to put it another way—take stock of himself.

Once the decision to change jobs is made, *"How To Market Yourself . . . Yourself!"* takes over. Ironically, there are many individuals who know how to market any product you can think of except one—themselves! And if the marketing executive needs help—then the engineer, accountant, lawyer, writer, or Indian Chief frequently needs help even more! The principles used in this book can be applied to literally any field of endeavor: It was purposely written this way.

1

Every manufactured product has to have a *method of distribution,* and so do you in your Job Campaign. You may elect to be distributed directly—through Want Ads, Direct Mail Campaign, or Telephone Campaign—or you may want to use a distributor, such as an Employment Agency or Executive Search firm.

Every facet of marketing yourself will be discussed, from the *Sales Literature* (your Resume) to the *Packaging* (your Appearance).

Over the past fourteen years I have been in both the Employment Agency and Executive Search business. I have developed various successful methods and techniques in placing and recruiting candidates. As President of my own Executive Search Firm I am involved daily in the job hiring process. I had *better know* just what it takes to get yourself hired by an employer!

I have drawn on these years of both "pitching" and recruiting candidates to provide me with the "firing line" experience to communicate to the reader. Because my business is exclusively *Executive Search*—which means we are hired and compensated by the companies we serve—I can afford to be completely candid with the reader. This book was *not* written as a sales tool to drum up Executive Guidance or Out Placement business.

When executives go through the job changing process, they are exposed to so many avenues or directions to head in that without having some sort of guide to weed out the dead ends, they are bound to waste a lot of both valuable time and money.

As in marketing, I have provided additional tools for your *primary* and *secondary research: Primary research* on how you can personally evaluate and check out your prospective employer— with his competitors, customers, and suppliers. This process, in itself, could lead to *additional* job offers. For secondary research, I have provided you with basic sources of research materials and directories, and also how and where to locate those special research materials and directories. As in marketing any other product, you must have good market research information.

You will be using the same basic tools and techniques that any successful employment counsellor or executive recruiter would use. The major difference being that you are only concerning yourself with one product . . . you! Nobody in the World has as much product knowledge about yourself—as you! Take advantage of it. . . .

When you market yourself—*yourself*—you are serving as your own marketing and employment consultant. As an alternative to paying thousands of dollars to an outside firm, *How To Market Yourself . . . Yourself!* should enable you to land that outstanding job, *yourself*, and save those thousands of dollars!

1 Analyze the Product . . . YOU!

Before determining what kind of job or opportunity you are seeking, you should take stock of yourself and try to answer the question, "Why do I feel like changing?" Maybe you really should *not* change.

Some years ago, an unmarried design engineer I recruited for a farm implements company located in a small Midwestern town, called me after one week on the job and said, "I have made a mistake. The job was wrong. The company was wrong, and the town was awful for a single guy." He wanted me to place him with any other company, just so long it was located in a big city. I told the young engineer, "A new job frequently has what is known as 'the period of adjustment', and after one week it certainly has not stood the test of time." We made an agreement that he would try to block out any negative thoughts about his situation, and try to do the best job he could for ninety days and then give me another telephone call. I assured him that if he did not at least *begin* to feel differently about his job and environment, I would place him with another company.

Shortly after the ninety days were up, he called me to report that his situation was beginning to improve. He felt his work was becoming meaningful, he had joined the company bowling league, and last but not least, he was seriously dating a girl. The irony is that he met this young woman in the laundromat near what he had referred to as his "crummy" apartment which lacked laundry facilities.

Nine years later my friend the engineer resigned his position, which was at that time Assistant Chief Engineer. He started his own company which supplies parts for the farm implement industry, and today is most successful and happy. I might also mention that his plant is located in that same little midwestern town and the girl he met in the laundromat is now his wife, and mother of their three children.

Any career change should have the *proper timing*. One week on the job does not quite make it! As in all life, timing is *so* important. In planning a career strategy, the length of time in the present position should be long enough to go from a liability to an asset.

If my engineering friend had just stayed a few months on the job, that time period would have been a liability, but by investing at least a couple of years in the position he was then able to market his experience.

Working environments are dynamic and frequently change. How one feels about one's position after just a short time certainly will not be the same in a couple of years.

One might even compare a new job to growing a garden. If you neglect it, chances are you will not be successful and will ultimately quit. Nurture it, develop it, make every effort to do well, and there is an excellent probability that your career, like your garden, will

6

flourish and reward you. Reward you with large dividends—both psychological and monetary.

Everyone has their ups and downs, good days and bad days. I always advise, when an individual indicates that he has had it with his job, that maybe he just needs a little vacation. I am truly amazed at the high percentage of lower, middle, and upper management people who do not take enough time off from their work. I advocated career dedication in the previous paragraphs, but burning one's self out is a fast way to career dissatisfaction!

Using the garden analogy: Too much water is no good, too much fertilizer is no good, too much of *anything* is no good—especially work!

I advocate a couple of short vacations during the year as compared to one long one.

A friend of mine is a stockbroker for a large New York Stock Exchange member firm. I will refer to him as Dave. For years, Dave hardly ever took a vacation. When he did, he would spend as much on long distance calls to his clients and office as he would for the resort he stayed at for two weeks.

Dave told me that he would send his wife off each day to the swimming pool and whatever other activities that were provided. He would eventually join her very coincidentally at about the time the market closed at 4 P.M. Eastern Standard Time. You would think that once every two or three years when he did take a vacation, he would have had sense enough to take a real one. This man literally worked seven days a week.

One day Dave complained of severe stomach pains, and was convinced by his wife to see their family physician. He had ulcers.

The doctor ordered Dave to cut down at work and to take periodic vacations—real ones with no business conducted. In fact, what the doctor suggested was that Dave and his wife go on a cruise for a couple of weeks where there would be no easy access to a telephone. Dave returned from that cruise indicating that he had not realized what he had been missing those past eighteen years. He had never really taken a vacation. (Work vacations, in my mind, are not really vacations.) Dave had a great time, felt wonderful, and looked a lot better—especially with a tan in February.

By following his doctor's orders, which were to watch his diet, cut down on smoking, cut down on hours worked, and periodic vacations (even if short ones) Dave recovered completely and was enjoying life a lot more within a year.

A peculiar thing happened when Dave cut down on his working hours. His commissions actually improved slightly. He apparently was beginning to work smarter rather than harder. There is very definitely a point of diminishing returns when you overwork.

2   **SELF-HELP JOB EVALUATION**

Job Fulfillment—or Lack of it

"I just do not *enjoy* my job anymore. . . ." Try to analyze why you feel this way. Is it really the job itself, or is it some other reason? Frequently, the other reasons can make you *think* it is the job itself.

I remember one of my clients calling me and telling me that their Chief Architect had suddenly quit—just like that! I will refer to this architect as Dan.

I had recruited Dan approximately six years earlier. The President of the company indicated that during the past six years of employment Dan had done an outstanding job. The President said, "Dan has never missed a day of work, never complained, and appeared quite happy." He went on to say, "Dan has almost tripled his salary during the past six years." The President seemed really baffled about the situation.

I immediately called Dan and asked, "What's happening?" Executives simply do not quit their jobs for no reason. There had to be an explanation. . . .

Dan finally leveled with me. After fifteen years of marriage, his wife had run off with another man. Dan felt he could solve his problem by quitting his job and running off to California. Dan apparently felt that he needed a new set of surroundings.

I am certainly no psychologist, but I felt that maybe what Dan needed was someone to talk things out with. He had no children, both his parents were dead, and he was an only child. After talking with me for a couple of hours, Dan admitted that he really loved his job. He also reasoned out that quitting a job he loved while going through a painful divorce made no sense at all.

Dan called the President and rejoined the company. At the President's urging, Dan did take an immediate three weeks vacation. Upon returning, he changed his surroundings by moving to another apartment.

Four years have gone by and today, I am happy to report, Dan is remarried, the father of a brand new baby boy, and still employed with the same company—only now as a Vice President.

All personal problems are obviously not that easily solved. The above example merely illustrates that one should not be too quick to quit a valued job: Especially when the real problem is totally unrelated.

When you really think about it, many times the job itself is quite stimulating and challenging. If the job itself measures up highly, one should stop right there—and try to figure out why you are even considering a change!

Yet every other aspect about a job could be A-1—Compensation, location, the people you work with—but if the job itself is dull, boring and miserable . . . that is the backbreaker!

If you truly consider your job stimulating, challenging, and enjoyable consider yourself blessed, and start counting your blessings!

Evaluating Your Compensation

Before you consider changing positions, think about the benefits you receive from earning a high salary. Money can bring a lot of joy and fulfillment into your life.

I read in the newspaper the other day of a school teacher who gave up his career to go to work in the coal mines of Kentucky at triple his teachers' salary. He was willing to sacrifice mental stimulation during the day for the benefits which high wages would bring to him and his family. Each one of us must set our own values and priorities.

I tell people who complain to conduct their own salary surveys. Answer some classified ads describing positions similar to your own. You just might be surprised to learn that your own salary is quite competitive. If, after checking out your salary with what other companies are paying, you find that your salary is competitive but you still want or need more money, then you might consider one of the following:

1. Increase Your Worth to Either Your Employer or a Competitor. This alternative may mean going back to school at night to obtain stronger academic credentials. Employees frequently are pleasantly surprised to find that when they do return to night school to prepare for a better job—their own company suddenly recognizes their talents and promotes them!

On more than one occasion, personnel directors have confided in me that their company "keeps an eye" on employees who are returning to night school. Employers realize that when additional

11

education is completed, if *they* do not take care of that ambitious employee . . . their competitors will.

It is pure economics and good business. Better to give their own employee the raise or promotion rightfully deserved than have that employee quit. Why be forced to go into the market place to replace him—paying even more for an unknown quantity.

2. Supplement Your Income. If everything else about your job is ideal except the pay, then, rather than change, obtain a second job working as many hours as appropriate. Another approach for a married couple to consider, when feasible, is for the wife to get a job or a better job. If you are not married, chances are you may not need the money that badly anyway. . . .

3. Have a Good Old-Fashion-Talk With The Boss. If you feel you are worth more—then convince your boss. But you had better use a little empathy ahead of time, and try to place yourself in his position. Are you really worth any more money? Before sitting down and having this "heart to heart" talk, the groundwork should be laid.

Again, timing is crucial! You might volunteer for some extra work for awhile, or make sure you are really putting in all those extra hours that you keep complaining about at home. In other words, make your boss's job a little easier and you just might be rewarded.

One special consideration has happened before in United States history and is beginning to be implemented again as this book is being written—*voluntary wage controls.*

Unfortunately you may be due for a raise but your employer, in order to adhere to the voluntary guidelines set down by the Federal Government, will either curtail all raises, or raises will be so minimal that they will not mean much.

Most likely, the only way to obtain a raise during a period of wage controls is to switch employers.

A word of caution though: Wage controls do not last for ever, and your employer may be able to make it up to you, at least partially, after the controls are lifted.

How Much Travel?

If travel in a job suddenly becomes a hardship, one should ask oneself, "Is it indefinite or temporary?" I have seen many executives all set to give up an otherwise satisfactory career merely because of a *temporary* change in their routine. Careful evaluation should be given before throwing away several self-fulfilling years with the same company over a few months of travel.

I know that there are outside family pressures created when a travel schedule does become hectic, but the family must be made aware that you are only away out of necessity—not enjoyment. One can try compensating for the time away during the week by spending extra time with the family on weekends. Unfortunately, too many traveling executives are gone Monday through Friday, and then spend their weekends playing golf, tennis, poker, or whatever, with friends rather than being with their families.

Our families warrant at least two-sevenths the time we devote to our jobs!

Too many male executives take for granted that their wives and families will automatically understand . . . sometimes yes, and sometimes no. You must take the time and make the effort to *make sure they understand.* The family must be made to feel that the entire family sometimes must make temporary sacrifices for even greater long term family rewards.

If too much travel becomes a permanent condition, then one should first consider obtaining a new position within the same company, before looking to the outside. It is amazing how many executives do not bother to analyze what else they could do *within their own company* before making up their minds to give up and go elsewhere.

Does Authority Equate to Responsibility?

In analyzing this problem of poorly balanced authority-responsibility, I have come across an interesting statistic. Many of the managers who make this complaint of their supervisors are even more guilty of the very same fault. There frequently seems to be a chain reaction with this problem.

My analysis is drawn from reference checks and by the candidates themselves.

One way to approach the problem is to set the tone by *example*. If the boss knows that you are bending over backwards to develop your own workers by delegating the appropriate authority and responsibility, he just might catch the "bug." Present it to him at the right time and in the appropriate manner. Do not *confront* him with a comparison illustrating that you are a better manager than he—but rather *explain* what you are doing to develop and promote your people. A positive approach can become contagious.

How to Obtain Additional Help From The Boss

Instead of just nagging the boss for more help and crying out that you are overworked and underpaid, you might try the following:

Outline *exactly* what you need in the way of additional help (do not overpad, the boss is not that dumb!).

Next, explain just what the additional help will do to increase productivity. It is the basic cliche, "It takes money to make money", but show him with facts and figures. You might also throw in a few charts and graphs. You want your boss to actually visualize the net benefit he will receive by giving you more help.

Commuting Time to Work

Discontent with the length of commuting time is very relative. To some, anything more than a twenty minute drive to the office is too

14

much. While others, especially in New York, think nothing of taking an hour and a half to commute to the office.

I have found that by simply changing the *mode* of transportation, the drudgery of a long commute may become more bearable. Try driving—then maybe changing to the train. It is amazing what you can accomplish on the commuter train: Work, read the newspaper, or even add a couple hours of sleep each day. Some prefer the car pool, even though your schedule has to be quite regimentated to participate.

I have frequently recommended moving closer to work, rather than give up on an otherwise good career. People frequently move across the country with less hesitation than moving twenty miles—just to make life more pleasant. There seems to be some sort of psychological block that says, "If you are not going to move at least a couple of hundred miles, then why move at all?"

Many people just do not like to travel medium or long distances to get to work. They would be ready to sacrifice almost anything just to be able to work close to home.

I, myself, have been at both ends of the spectrum. For years I commuted an hour and fifteen minutes, doorstep to doorstep, in the morning and evening. This was a total of two and a half hours commuting time per day. In recent years I have moved my office to within ten minutes driving time from my home. It sure is nice to leave the house at 7:50 A.M. and arrive at the office at 8:00 A.M.

One does not have much difficulty in finding productive use for an extra couple of hours a day!

Job Promotion Strategy

Frequently, we have to pay our so-called "dues" in order to get ahead. There are many careers where one has to work for a low salary and do mundane chores in the beginning. These sacrifices are made in order to achieve the ultimate goal—the pinnacle of career or profession. The drudgery becomes a lot less uncomfortable when we have meaningful goals to shoot for.

You sometimes have to help your supervisor make the decisior that you are ready for promotion. Frequently, the best way to do this is to help your boss get promoted. Make The Boss look good whenever possible. Let him or her know that you want more work. Offer to give extra assistance. Volunteer for other additional assignments. Or, when all else fails, discreetly mention his name as a possible candidate the next time the friendly executive headhunter calls you!

How Good Are The Fringe Benefits?

If the pay is high enough, an employee can create his own fringe benefit program.

In fact, Uncle Sam provides for those individuals who are not covered by a qualified or government retirement plan a chance to set up their own personal retirement funds. This program is called Individual Retirement Account (IRA).

Even nonworking spouses are eligible to contribute to an IRA. You could have two separate IRAs, one for you and one for your spouse.

Although there are various rules and regulations pertaining to IRAs—such as the amount you can contribute, deductions from your taxes each year, when you can withdraw the funds, etc.—but the ultimate retirement benefit gained when you participate is well worth the effort.

One could easily set up an IRA with a bank, savings and loan association, or insurance company. Institutions which provide IRA services will gladly provide you with all the necessary information.

Further information on IRAs is also provided by the Internal Revenue Service.

Some companies provide fringe benefits for their employees which total up to one-third or more of their salaries. When you think about it, they sure add up. If you had to duplicate, on your own, the fringe benefits which are provided for you by your employer—you just might get a rude awakening.

Such items as non-contributory pension plans, major medical coverage, life insurance, disability income insurance, tuition reimbursement, several weeks paid vacation, stock purchase plan—all add up to a substantial amount.

Depending on your position, and the company, you may also be receiving a company car, employee discount on merchandise, stock options, and perhaps a country club membership.

Fringe benefits are obviously not everything, and, as already pointed out, if other qualities and the salary of your job are high you can purchase many of them for yourself. But they certainly are expensive.

How Important is Climate?

If you spend a lot of free time enjoying recreational activities available only because you live in a particularly suitable climate, then you may miss this environment in another part of the country.

Snow-mobiling in Florida is not so good—and the beaches of North Dakota in winter are less than adequate!

Many people make career sacrifices just so they can enjoy a particular climate.

No climate is perfect: It just appears that some are less perfect than others.

Sometimes I hear people say, "I've had it with this lousy cold weather", and they take off for the Sun Belt. Sometimes they stay, other times they return. Be careful not to blame the weather instead of some other factors which are really troubling you. There appears to be a coincidence in that when executives express most disgust with their climate, at the same time things are usually not going well with their jobs, or they are having problems at home.

An exception to the above is when you or a member of your family has a genuine health problem. Thus, it could become imperative that you move to a healthier climate.

Can You Stay Too Long With One Employer?

The answer is both yes and no. *Yes,* if you are not progressing within the company, both career-wise and salary-wise. It is easy to become complacent in your job when the company is not treating you badly—just a *little bit badly.* It does not hurt to take an interview with another company *every* couple of years or so. If nothing else, you might find out that the grass is *not* always greener on the other side of the fence, and you just might appreciate what you have that much more.

No—if you are making good progress within your own company. You never want to change jobs just for the sake of changing. If you look forward to going to work each morning, and know you are compensated fairly—then count your blessings. . . .

I frequently hear comments such as, "I could not conceivably consider changing jobs. After all, I am forty-five years old and I've been employed here for over twenty years. I must think about my pension." What a lot of people do not realize is that with the advent of the Employee Retirement Income Security Act of 1974, otherwise known as ERISA, the incentive to stay with one employer for many years could be reduced. From a pension standpoint alone, because of ERISA, it is now theoretically possible to collect more money at retirement from equally dividing up your employment lifetime between two employers; rather than just staying with one employer an entire working lifetime. The caveat is that there would have to be a particular set of circumstances in order for this to occur. The two companies would have to have pension plans which vested and payed out just at a certain percentage rate. Prior to ERISA, this possibility was greatly reduced. Too many companies required too many years to become fully vested.

When considering your present pension plan in relation to a prospective employer's—wanting to know the consequences of a job change strictly from a pension standpoint—I would advise consulting an Employee Benefits Specialist before making any final decision. It may take some time, and there may be a fee involved, but your retirement is too important, and there is too much at stake, not to have it checked and analyzed professionally.

The Working Environment

"The boss is really a great guy." "The people I work with are my friends." "The top management really have the employees' interests at heart." If one feels sentiments similar to the above, then that is *another* reason to stop and evaluate *why* you really want to make a change.

There is nothing like getting up in the morning and actually being anxious to get to work to be with people you enjoy and respect!

3 CREATING THE RESUME

Sounds easy enough—and it is. As simple as it is, though, an abundance of executives, including many in top level positions, just do not bother to put together a first class resume. Their credentials may be impeccable, but their resumes are strictly "bush league."

An outstanding resume is extremely important in making a job change. To someone who does not know you—you can only be judged by the quality of your resume.

We should view our resumes as our own sales representatives. These representatives had better look sharp and convey our message well!

Following are some suggestions for putting together an excellent resume:

Do Not Be Cheap—Use Good Paper. Cheap paper makes a very poor first impression. Why mess around? For the amount of paper you will need, you can afford excellent quality. I recommend 24 lb. heavyweight cotton (25%) fibre content. Also, make sure the envelopes match the paper. If not exactly the same, the envelope must still coordinate with the paper—as a sportcoat with pants.

Have the Resume Professionally Printed—Do Not Use Your Kid's Portable Typewriter. There is a world of difference between a resume typed on a portable typewriter and reproduced on your typical office copier, and one typed perfectly on an electric executive type typewriter then brought to a printer to be reproduced professionally.

The difference might be compared to a tailor-made suit versus one purchased very cheaply in a discount store. Both suits will cover your back, but one should look a whole lot better.

If neither you, nor anyone you know, is an excellent typist, then have your resume typed professionally. Your resume should look perfect!

Do Not Be Cute—No Crazy Colored Paper or Family Pictures. In most cases I am against using pictures in a resume, especially family pictures (who cares what your dog looks like in front of the fireplace with you, your wife, and your five kids?).

Make the employer or his executive search firm invite you in for an interview if they want to see what you look like. If you are ugly . . . give your charming personality a chance to work. If you think you are the handsome "macho" looking type . . . remember, the guy evaluating your resume may be ugly and resent your attributes, at least until he sits down to meet you, and finds out what a regular guy you are.

Go to the trouble to obtain the right quality paper: Use white or something very close. This business about bright paper attracting attention when compared with a stack of other resumes may work for a creative writing position, but for most others it may be offensive, and why take the chance?

Resume Chronology—First, Be Personal. Let the reader know who is being evaluated. At the top of every resume should be your *personal data*. Include such information as: Your name, address, and telephone number (do not forget the area code).

On the subject of *age:* I feel that this information should be included in your resume whether you are nineteen or ninety-nine. Even though an employer cannot discriminate because of age (they would be in direct violation of both Federal and State age discrimination laws), by omitting your age you are simply telling the employer you are old, and do not want to reveal it. Furthermore, an employer can simply add the years of experience to when you graduated from school and figure your age.

Always write *"Date of Birth"* rather than your actual present age. It avoids updating. You are liable to celebrate another birthday, and you do not want the reader to know how long you have really been looking, do you?

The *Marital Status* should be exactly that: If you are divorced, then specify "Divorced", and not "Single."

When a candidate is checked out and has specified "single," and an employer finds he or she was previously married, that becomes a "red flag." It makes little difference that the prospective employee may have innocently interpreted it as a matter of semantics.

Height and Weight are optional. If you are of proportional height and weight, then list the information. If you are five feet five inches tall, and weigh 250 lbs.—then I would omit height and weight from the resume. Height and weight help the reader draw a mental picture of you. If it is not going to be favorable then make him interview you, and give yourself the opportunity to charm him.

Do not include your *religion* on your resume. In this day and age, with stringent Federal laws, there is very little discrimination against any particular religion. I see no point in calling attention to the fact that you are of a specific religion.

Indicating whether you are *male or female* is also unnecessary—unless you happen to have a first name that could belong to either a male or female.

Do not list any *racial or ethnic description* of yourself. Again, let the employer interview you face-to-face. If you insist on telling the reader that you are a "minority," you may never get the interview. On the other hand, you may be the minority member who is qualified for the position and whom the employer wants to hire once he has met you.

If your *health* is excellent—then say so. If it is not so good—do not advertise it on a resume. If you have a physical handicap that does not interfere with your ability to do your job, then do not list it. Do not go out of your way to create a negative picture.

There is nothing wrong with highlighting the positives on a resume—but *never lie!* Not only is it immoral and dishonest to lie on a resume, but just plain stupid. When writing a resume, go on the assumption that the information will be verified and checked out. Chances are it really will be, and any misstatement will soon catch up with you.

Some years ago my firm recruited a district sales manager for a building products company. I will refer to him as Lee. The company had a policy of doing their own reference checking, so we cannot take credit for what I am about to describe.

Lee was working as district sales manager for a competitor at the time we recruited him. He was thirty years old and had worked for his firm for four years. Previously, Lee had been with a smaller company in the same industry which went bankrupt. He had worked for them for two years.

Lee had indicated that he had an M.B.A. and a B.S.M.E. from two top Eastern universities. Lee also indicated that he was an All-Ivy League tennis player while in school.

Every year my client has a National Sales Meeting at a different resort. Three months after Lee joined my client, while attending the sales meeting, the vice president of sales invited him to play tennis. Now, the vice president indicated that some years earlier he had been cut from the tennis squad of the same university where Lee had been a star player.

The vice president completely dominated Lee in their tennis match. Lee was so outclassed that the vice president asked him again what year he was All-Ivy League.

When they all returned, the vice president just could not convince himself that he had so completely outplayed an All-Ivy tennis player who was twenty years younger than he.

He personally called the university to verify Lee's record. Not only had Lee lied about being All-Ivy, he was not even on a tennis team! He never graduated from that school! Lee never even took a single course there!

The university where Lee was supposed to have received his M.B.A. also indicated that they had never heard of him. The vice president called Lee into his office and confronted him.

Lee at first tried to bluff his way out, but finally broke down and admitted that he never went to college at all. In fact, he never finished his last year of high school. All the time Lee was supposed to be in school, he was actually atgking for his father, who was a builder. Lee was obviously very bright, and well-read about the construction business.

Lee knew about the company that went bankrupt, so he took advantage of the information, and Presto! Lee instantly became a District Sales Manager of that company before it had folded. Lee figured that no one would bother checking with a bankrupt company. Lee was right. The company he was working for at the time we recruited him had never reference-checked him. In fact my client's personnel department, which insists upon doing all their own reference checking, had not yet checked Lee out.

The irony of the situation was that the vice president called Lee's former employer, and their vice president of sales reported that Lee had done a terrific job during his four years of employment. Only, he thought Lee was an All-Ivy *hockey* player. . . .

During the three months Lee had been with my client, the vice president admitted he had done an excellent job. But much as the vice president hated to do it, he felt that he could not tolerate having one of his managers less than completely honest. He could not completely trust Lee, and would always hold that against him. Lee was fired.

Job Objectives—*Careful, They Can Hurt You.* A few years back, I remember a young salesman, two years out of school, attempting to change companies with absolutely no results. I will refer to him as Pete.

Pete had sent out literally hundreds of resumes without a "nibble." As a favor to his father, who is a friend of mine, I went over Pete's resume.

There was only one thing wrong—but what a "whale" of a mistake. His stated job objective was "sales management." With only two years experience, and the first nine months of that spent inside the plant learning the business, this young man felt he was ready for management. Questioned about his job objective, Pete explained that *ultimately* sales management was his goal. He explained, also, that any reader of his resume would surely realize that no one is ready to become a sales manager in the steel industry after just fifteen months of field-sales experience.

Pete immediately understood my line of questioning, and realized the mistake he had made. His Job Objective on his resume should have stated his intended immediate goal. The Objective should have been *Salesman*—and not *Sales Manager.* Do not fall into the trap of *assuming* the reader of your resume will know what you *really* mean. Be explicit.

Pete was also very interested in considering other industries for career possibilities. But who would know this, unless it was spelled-out in the Job Objective? His Job Objective made no reference to the fact that Pete would consider other industries.

Job Objectives should be one of the following:

A. *Extremely General.* Here, you would want to cover just about anything and everything. An example: Pete might have had as a Job Objective, "Professional sales position within either the steel industry, or an industry which could utilize my two years sales experience in the steel industry."

B. *Very Specific.* This approach can only be done effectively on a customized basis. Each resume must have a specific Job Objective aimed at whatever particular position you are seeking.

An example in the area of advertising and brand management: If you would consider several related areas, then print some resumes aimed at brand management, brand advertising, or sales promotion. You might also print some aimed at the advertising agency side of the business.

Resumes aimed at specific positions are frequently and successfully used. The only negative is the added printing cost, and that is really insignificant when you consider just how much is at stake.

C. *No Job Objective.* If an individual is genuinely "wide open" about what he or she might do, then instead of having a Job Objective which is so broad as to not really *be* a Job Objective, simply skip it. Whatever position you apply for will then become your Job Objective.

Education. Education should either be up-front, after Personal Data, or at the very end of the resume. The key question—whether or not you have a good education.

If you are a high school dropout, or an honors graduate from Harvard, the answer becomes rather obvious. If you are somewhere in between, then you should ask yourself, "Are my educational credentials an asset or a liability to my resume?" You must be your own judge.

The reader of a resume with poor academic credentials prominently listed may toss it aside before he finds out that your twenty years experience is exactly what the company is looking for!

List your highest level of academic attainment first. If it is a graduate degree, then that should be at the top. If your only degree is a Bachelor of Science, then begin with that.

Grade point averages should be listed only when they are *worth* highlighting. If you received all Cs—then omit grades from the resume. If you happen to be a Phi Beta Kappa—then by all means let the reader know. Never lie—"If you've got it, flaunt it"—if not, keep quiet.

Do not list a high school diploma, unless that is all you have. An exception might be made if you graduated with such outstanding honors that you really should include them.

I generally do not recommend listing partially completed *graduate* degrees. Half a Masters Degree and fifty cents maybe gets you on the bus. A partially completed graduate degree can also label you a "quitter." However, if you did not complete a Bachelor's Degree, but have a couple of years of credits under your belt—indicate as much. A year or two of college sounds so much better than "just a high school graduate."

Military.   If you were an officer in the military, especially if your total other work experience is limited, definitely list it right up-front, under Education—assuming your education is strong enough to be up-front. On the other hand, if your education is weak, but you possess an outstanding Military record—then you have to use good judgment in constructing the resume. You might list Military Experience right under Personal Data and Education at the end. Generally, where one has a number of years of job experience, the Military experience could almost be eliminated from the resume. It depends on how much room you have, and how significant your years in the military were.

EXPERIENCE—The "Meat and Potatoes".   Now, down to what the employer determines you can do for him. *This is the part of the resume that can "make or break" you.*

To begin with, always list your *last position first*. The reader doesn't care if you worked your way through college twenty years ago mowing lawns . . . if he has to read through much superfluous information before he gets to reasons for hiring today, he is liable to get bored and toss your resume aside.

The one exception to listing your last position first would be when the experience of most importance to the reader is not in your most recent position.

If you are applying for, or being considered for, a position as plant manager of a food plant, and you spent the last two years traveling around the country trying to break into show business as a singer, but the prior ten years were spent running food plants— then it becomes obvious which experience you want the reader to see first.

Experience should, generally, be positioned on the front page of the resume, just below Education and/or Military. An exception might be made when the individual has very little experience, but outstanding Education, Honors, and Miscellaneous.

In listing your present position, always include the date you began until present. By using the word "present" instead of today's date you avoid creating a rapidly outdated resume; "to present" might have been written a year ago, but if nothing significant has changed, the resume is still perfectly acceptable. If you had used the current date a year ago, your resume is outdated.

Be very precise in writing the names of all your employers. You may know them by their initials, but the reader may not. This is especially true if you are being considered for a position outside your industry. Also, indicate the exact division you work for. If you worked for General Motors, it could make a difference if you were a design engineer for the Diesel Engine Division, as opposed to the Pontiac Car Division.

Your job title should also be exact. No abbreviations. If the Job Title is something that the reader might not readily understand, then include an explanation of just what it means. This is usually necessary when you want to transfer your skills from a technical position to something outside your industry.

The description of exactly what you do on your job should be brief, but paint a picture of just what your employer pays you to do everyday. Do not be afraid to list any significant accomplishments in your present and past positions. Keep in mind that you want to create the impression of an employee who is making positive contributions to his job—and demonstrating individual career development along the way.

A word of caution: "Do not blow smoke." If you were part of a *team* which made a significant contribution, then indicate so. Do not fail to mention "it was a team effort," then try to give the reader the impression that without *you* . . . the company would fold. Sincere honesty has a way of showing through.

Illustrate, in describing your duties, just where you fit into the table of organization at your present and past employers. Indicate to whom, and in what capacity, you report; and who reports to you.

You may or may not want to include a reason for leaving. If you were recruited by an executive search firm—why advertise that you were looking anyway and could be gotten cheaply? If the reason you would consider another position is at least neutral, and preferably positive, then by all means include a reason for leaving.

A neutral reason would be where a company was going out of business. It is not your fault—at least I hope not—but it is not a feather in your cap either.

If the reason for changing is better opportunity, new challenge, or desire for next level of responsibility, then I see nothing wrong with indicating so.

Never use negative reasons for leaving. If the reason *is* negative—you are doing a lousy job and want to leave before you get fired—then just omit any reason for leaving.

Never downgrade your present employer or sing "The Old Sour Grapes Song." This will really turn-off the resume reader.

Again, we come down to the positive impression we want to make on whoever is evaluating the resume.

Other Awards and Honors—Miscellaneous. These are catch-all categories to be used when they apply. Generally, they are at the end of the resume. An exception would be made for an individual who is long on awards and honors, but short on experience.

If you have received an outstanding award—scholastic, public service, athletic, social, etc., by all means mention it.

Association, organization, or society memberships should only be included if they truly are something special to belong to. Examples would be professional associations whose memberships are comprised of doctors, engineers, lawyers, etc. The association, organization, or society should exemplify something very positive, and focus on the high achievement of the individual who belongs. Do not list any group which could possibly antagonize a reader.

Under Miscellaneous, be practical in listing hobbies and other interests. Also, be brief. The reader might not be interested in all the ribbons and trophies you have won showing your champion cocker spaniel.

Money—Pleasant Subject, But Avoid It On The Resume. I rarely recommend stating your present salary on a resume. If the reader wants to know—let him ask.

Your present salary may be lower than the reader supposes. Why help your future employer reduce your starting salary? There may be a bonus or a significant profit sharing payment in addition to your salary. There may also be a host of fringe benefits that your present employer provides.

Your present salary may be higher than the reader wants to pay. Why knock yourself out of the box without giving yourself the opportunity to convince him that it would be in his company's best interest to pay more for the job. Maybe the employer is not aware of what the competition is currently paying for the same job. I feel that the personal interview is the time to discuss salary, or at least on the telephone where you can discuss the subject back and forth.

Do not indicate desired salary on your resume because there is no way to include every factor to be considered in setting this desired salary without going into a long dissertation.

Some positions you would accept for a lot less money than others. Some positions offer greater opportunities than others. Some have bonuses while others do not. Some companies have terrific fringe benefit programs, while others have practically none. Some companies would require a relocation to an undesirable area, while others are located close to home or in a very attractive area. Some positions require extensive traveling. Some companies are located where it would require long and expensive commuting every day. Some companies offer terrific opportunities for salary and career growth while others may only offer an attractive starting salary. Some company working environments are much more pleasant than others.

Salary desired, like present salary, should be discussed in a personal interview.

References.   References should *not* be given in the resume. Again, let the reader come to you and ask. Why have valuable references bothered unnecessarily by someone who may have no real interest in hiring you.

Unfortunately, references are contacted for reasons other than they should be. An example would be for a possible employer to check a reference just to "pick the brain" of the reference about his own company. Your reference check could be a perfect excuse to call a competitor and see how they are doing.

If you must answer a blind ad, absolutely do not use any references. You would be leaving yourself wide open for problems, and never know who the culprit was!

Selection of references should be given a great deal of consideration before the final choices are made. Everyone expects a good reference, so you had better make sure that yours come through for you.

References could very easily make or break you. You must check beforehand with each reference you cite to obtain their permission.

If there is a reference or two that you must use, such as a former supervisor, but have doubts about, then have a trusted friend conduct a "test run" before you actually give his name as a reference. Your friend could pose as an executive recruiter who is screening a candidate for his client. It is better to have your reference "bum rap" you to a friend than to a real employer.

What you might do afterwards is call that former supervisor and indicate that you were turned down for an outstanding position right after he was called to give you a reference. Tell him that you are now a finalist for another position and hope you can count on him to give you a good reference. Usually, a former employer confronted with the fact that you are aware that he cost you one job opportunity, will go easier on you the next time around. People usually only "bum rap" others when they think they can get away with it. Once they are confronted they usually mellow and come through with a decent reference.

If, when confronted, the former supervisor shows no remorse or blatantly denies that he ever gave you a bad reference, then you had better avoid using him for a reference—period! Use someone else.

Giving glowing references for an individual can quickly grow tiresome. It is time-consuming and could be a nuisance, especially if there are frequent interruptions during important meetings.

Try to have a valuable reference receive the least possible number of calls to still accomplish what you want—that is, getting hired by a new employer. At the conclusion of your resume should be the statement: "References will be furnished upon request."

Some examples of effective resumes follow.

John A. Doe
222 Maple Street
Anytown, U.S.A.
Telephone 213-555-1212

JOB OBJECTIVE

General Manager or Multiplant Management in the Food Industry.

PERSONAL

Born September 10, 1926 - Married - Three Children - Height 5' 11" - Weight 190 lbs.

EDUCATION

B.S. - Industrial Engineering - Purdue University - Graduated June 1948 - Maintained "B" Average.

EXPERIENCE

1/72 TO PRESENT

MAJOR FIRM

Plant Manager - Frozen Foods Division

Joined Company as Plant Manager. Responsible for 350 employees - 29 Million in sales. Report to Vice-President of Division. Responsible for following functions: Operations - Engineering - Accounting - Quality Control - Traffic and Distribution - Industrial Relations.

Originally joined company when plant employed 250 employees and produced 15 million in sales. By maintaining costs and efficiency, we were able to nearly double sales and profits - while increasing costs by only two-thirds.

1/52 TO 1/72

MAJOR FIRM

9/67 TO 1/72 - Director of Industrial Engineering

Responsible for Corporate Industrial Engineering function of 100 Million Dollar Food Company. Supervise a Corporate Staff of four Industrial Engineers plus give functional direction to five Plant Industrial Engineers.

9/63 TO 9/67 - Plant Superintendent - Frozen Food Plant

Responsible for 3 General Foremen - 9 Foremen - and 180 Hourly Employees. Responsible for all Production - Production Planning and Control. Reported to Plant Manager.

8/60 TO 9/63 - General Foreman - Frozen Food Plant

Responsible for 3 Foremen and 60 Production Employees.

6/58 TO 8/60 - Corporate Staff Industrial Engineer

Functionally responsible for 3 Plant Industrial Engineers. Covered all phases of Industrial Engineering.

6/56 TO 6/58 - Foreman - Frozen Food Plant

Responsible for 20 Production Employees.

1/52 TO 6/56 - Plant Industrial Engineer - Frozen Food Plant

Responsible for Incentives - Time Study - Standards - Layout - Equipment Justification. Worked with vendors in equipment selection. Reported directly to Plant Manager. Worked in plant employing approximately 300 people.

6/48 TO 6/52	United States Army

Honorable Discharge with the rank of Captain. Primarily assigned as Supply Officer in both the U.S. and Japan.

MISCELLANEOUS   Member of Lions International - American Legion - Manage Little League baseball team - enjoy jazz - golf.

REFERENCES   References Furnished Upon Request.

John J. Doe
123 Elm Street
Anytown, U.S.A.
Telephone - 312-555-1212

JOB OBJECTIVE
Corporate Controller or Financial Officer of Major Firm

PERSONAL
Born September 21, 1941 - Married - Three Children - Height 6' 0" - Weight 175 lbs.

EDUCATION
MBA - University of Chicago - Graduated June 1965 - Majored in Finance - Graduated with Distinction

BS - Business Administration - University of Illinois - Majored in Accounting - Graduated with High Honors

CPA - State of Illinois - November 1965

EXPERIENCE

8/74 TO PRESENT
MAJOR FIRM

7/75 TO Present - Division Controller - Widget Division

Responsible for complete controllership function for 200 million dollar division. Supervise a department of 300. Reporting to me are the Assistant Controller, Audit Manager, Financial Analysis Manager, Budget Manager, Cost Manager, and the Data Processing Manager. I report directly to the Division Vice-President.

In two years, my department's costs were reduced by 30 percent. This was accomplished with the help of some outstanding subordinates.

8/74 TO 7/75 - Assistant Controller - Widget Division

Joined above Division as number-two man before being promoted.

8/70 TO 8/74	**ACME CORPORATION**
	Corporate Internal Audit Manager

Joined firm as first Corporate Internal Audit Manager they ever employed. Was hired to set up Corporate Internal Audit Department. Wrote the Audit Policy and Procedure Manual which is currently in use. Built department from scratch to a complement of eight professionals when I left.

Was hired directly from Major CPA Firm where I served as outside Audit Manager for Employer.

9/65 TO 8/70	**MAJOR CPA FIRM**
	7/68 TO 8/70 - Audit Manager

Responsible for major audit clients - Supervised a staff of up to nineteen professionals. Reported to a Firm Partner.

9/66 TO 7/68 - Senior Auditor

Served as Group Leader reporting to Audit Manager for various clients.

9/65 TO 9/66 - Staff Auditor

First year on Audit Staff. Assisted in client engagements - reported to a Senior Auditor.

MISCELLANEOUS	Member of the Society of Certified Public Accountants. Treasurer of Local School Board 999. Licensed pilot. Enjoy gourmet cooking.
REFERENCES	References Furnished Upon Request.

Susan J. Doe
456 Elm Street
Anytown, U.S.A.
Telephone 212-555-1212

JOB OBJECTIVE

Group Product Manager or Marketing Manager of packaged goods company.

PERSONAL

Born September 1, 1948 - Single - Height 5′ 6″ - Weight 125 lbs.

EDUCATION

MBA - Harvard University - Graduated June 1972 - Majored in Marketing

BA - Roosevelt University - Graduated June 1970 - Majored in Mathematics

EXPERIENCE

7/75 TO PRESENT

MAJOR COMPANY

Brand Manager - Toiletries Division

Responsible for development of Division Marketing Strategy - Sales Forecasting - Division Marketing Budgets - Product Distribution - Product Advertising and Promotion.

Division responsibility for all new products from conception to national distribution. Profit and sales responsibility for existing lines of hair spray - 50 million dollars in sales and 5 million dollar advertising budget.

Supervise two Assistant Brand Managers and a Secretary.

7/72 TO 7/75

MAJOR COMPANY

1/74 TO 7/75 - Product Manager Household Products Division

Managed a product line of household products representing 15 million dollars in sales. Was responsible for national distribution for two new products.

<u>7/72 TO 1/74</u> - Assistant Product Manager

Joined firm as Assistant Product Manager directly from Business School. Assisted in managing six household products with sales totaling 120 million.

<u>MISCELLANEOUS</u>   Secretary of local chapter of American Marketing Association - Collect antiques - Enjoy classical music and mountain climbing.

<u>REFERENCES</u>   References Furnished Upon Request.

John E. Doe
1011 Elm Street
Anytown, U.S.A.
Telephone 219-555-1212

PERSONAL

Born September 3, 1936 - Married - Three Children - Height 5′ 11″ - Weight 160 lbs.

EDUCATION

PhD. - Physical Chemistry - M.I.T. - Graduated June - 1963

M.S. - Physical Chemistry - M.I.T. - Graduated June - 1960

B.S. - Physical Chemistry - M.I.T. - Graduated June - 1958

EXPERIENCE

6/63 TO PRESENT

MAJOR CHEMICAL COMPANY

6/75 TO Present - Director of Research and Development

Responsible for corporate new products and product support - All Research & Development functions.

Major responsibilities are: Product Development - Quality Control - Environmental Chemistry - Analytical Services and Staff Development.

Have total supervision for a staff of 82.

9/70 TO 6/75 - Associate Director New Product Development and Product Research

Total responsibility for all aspects of New Product Development - Product Research and Quality Control. Supervised a staff of 46.

6/67 TO 9/70 - Quality Control Manager

Responsible for all Quality Control Functions - Supervised staff of 18.

<u>6/63 TO 6/67</u> - Senior Research Chemist

Project Leader for New Product Development and Product Research.

<u>MISCELLANEOUS</u>   Member of Town Board of Trustees - Teach Chemistry at the local Junior College - Enjoy swimming - camping - and square dancing.

<u>REFERENCES</u>   References - Publications - Patents - and Memberships - are available upon request.

JOHN H. DOE

HOME ADDRESS	PERSONAL
789 Elm Street	Married
Anytown, U.S.A.	Height 5′ 8″
Telephone 305-555-1212	Weight 170 lbs.
	Born - 9/2/50

JOB OBJECTIVE To join a Corporate Legal Department.

EDUCATION J.D. - Northwestern University Law School - Graduated June 1976. Member of Northwestern University Law Review.

B.S. - University of Minnesota - Majored in History. Awarded Phi Beta Kappa - Graduated June 1973.

EXPERIENCE

7/76 TO PRESENT MAJOR LAW FIRM

Associate Attorney

Experience emphasis in the areas of SEC filings, mergers and acquisitions, divestitures, liquidations, Federal and State taxes, financing, and other general corporate legal problems. Have also had some concentration in drafting employee benefit plans.

SUMMER OF 1975 MAJOR LAW FIRM - LAW CLERK

Spent summer as assistant to Senior Partner in charge of taxes. My duties involved primarily tax and legal research.

MISCELLANEOUS Enjoy reading - playing guitar - fencing.

Member - Illinois State Bar

REFERENCES References Furnished Upon Request.

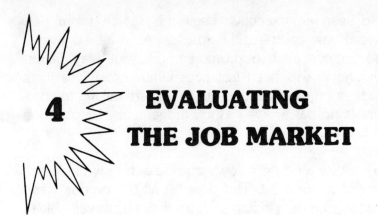

4 EVALUATING THE JOB MARKET

You might begin by looking in your own back yard.

Occasionally I am told, "If there was anything going on in my industry, I would surely know about it." My reply is, "You do not know what is under the rock until you lift it up and look under it." Contact your competitors—write to them—call them up—let them know you are available. Of course, if you do not want your present employer to know your intentions, then much discretion will have to be used. Anytime you contact a prospective employer, or take someone into your confidence, there is the possibility that word may leak back to your employer. The odds are in your favor ... but it is still a calculated risk.

"You will never get a base hit—unless you step up to the plate and take a swing."

I have also seen an executive begin his search for a new employer—word leaks back—and before he knows it he is given a raise, and sometimes even a promotion! Do not play games though. There have also been instances when executives were fired because their employer found out they were talking to competitors. There is no pat answer. Good judgement and common sense should prevail.

If one is to look for a new employer outside of his own industry, one again should make a list. This time list all the products and services related to your own industry. You will not be as valuable to any other company as to one that can immediately utilize your particular skills. You will also be amazed at how long that list can become.

When I receive a company search assignment, I always make not only a list of the competitors to go to searching for candidates, but of the adjunct industries as well.

A change to a totally different industry is actually quite easy for some professions. Examples would be accounting or data processing. These skills are relatively easy to transfer.

Most of the time, however, very serious thought should be given before switching industries. For most occupations switching industries can be difficult.

Is the reason you want to switch industries really the business you are in, or just your own particular environment? I frequently hear, "I *have* to get into another business or industry. This business just is not good anymore." If one has any length of time at all in a given profession within an industry—think three times, not twice, before giving it up!

In many industries and occupations, once you leave for any length of time, it becomes extremely difficult to get back in. I am not advocating never changing career directions or industries—but carefully weigh the downside risk.

An illustration of this point would be a data processing manager I know, whom I will refer to as John. John spent fifteen years with a major midwestern bank working his way up from programmer to data processing manager. He had joined the bank right out of college and had spent his entire professional life with them.

After fifteen years of continual gradual growth, and at the age of thirty-seven, John decided to leave the bank and go into business for himself.

What may have prompted this, was that he was in competition with two other managers for a promotion . . . and he did not receive it. The colleague who received the promotion was the only one of the three who had obtained an M.B.A. In fact, he had just completed it six months earlier, at night.

John decided to purchase a pizza restaurant franchise. He used his savings, his bank accumulated profit sharing, and borrowed a little from his father.

After struggling over a two year period—six and seven days a week—many hours a day—John decided he had made a mistake. The pizza business was losing money and John was miserable. He finally closed the restaurant and took a very substantial financial loss.

After searching to get back into data processing management for several months, he finally landed a position with an insurance company. His new job was equivalent to one level lower than the job he left at the bank some thirty months earlier. He also was earning ten percent less.

The field of data processing is so dynamic that being totally removed from it for 2½ years created some very significant hurdles for John to overcome.

Also, he returned to the job market in 1970, when few companies were expanding. In 1967, when John left, he felt that the economy was great, which it was, and that he would have no difficulty getting back into data processing if the pizza business did not work out. This is where he made his miscalculation. The economy entered a downturn, and he had become "rusty" in his original profession.

If you have been studying for some time, either at night school or part-time for a new industry or occupation, you have removed a substantial amount of the downside risk. You have become familiar with your prospective opportunity just by becoming prepared for it.

I know a police officer in a major city whom I will refer to as Phillip. Phillip attended law school at night over a period of several years. When he completed his law degree he went to work for the States Attorney's Office in his home town.

He gave up seven years of police work to pursue a career in law. This was a substantial change for Phillip, but he prepared for it well over a period of several years. He reduced his downside risk by the amount of preparation he went through to qualify himself. He also gave himself several years to change his mind. He did not risk his career on the police force until he had successfully passed his State Bar Examination.

Make sure you really understand your own reasons and motives for wanting to make substantial changes in your career, industry, or occupation. You may be able to fool the outside world, but you are on very thin ice when you try to fool yourself!

Some years ago a Roman Catholic priest was referred to me by a friend. The priest (I will call him James) had made up his mind to leave the priesthood. James indicated that after fifteen years as a priest, he wanted to give it all up to enter industry. He indicated that he thought he would be happier doing some sort of personnel work.

Eventually, a friend of his made a job for him with his company as a personnel supervisor. Unfortunately, James left the company after being on the job about six months. James had about three more jobs over the next two years. One more in personnel, one as a math instructor in a private school, and his third was as a real estate salesman.

James had got married within a year of leaving the priesthood. Apparently, he had known the girl he married for several years.

The speculation was that James was not unhappy being a parish priest. Our mutual friend felt that James left the priesthood because he wanted to marry his wife. He thought he would solve the problem by simply switching careers.

After his real estate job did not work out, James separated from his wife and headed out for California. That is the last I ever heard from him.

Make a list of all the positive reasons for going into a new industry. I frequently hear, "Well, that industry has many more opportunities than my own." I only suggest that you find out *why* it does. Talk to others working in the prospective industry.

Call a stock broker to send you some research material on the industry. Stock brokers can be quite helpful in analyzing an industry. They usually have excellent resource materials at their disposal.

Go to your local library and ask the reference librarian just what suggestions she might have in checking out an industry. I have found that reference librarians, when approached in the right manner, will go to great lengths to assist you.

Now, make a list of all the negative reasons for switching industries. How do you know you will even be happy in that new industry? Weigh the positives and negatives: If the positives strongly prevail—then switch industries.

Do not forget to consider your resume chronology. Have you switched industries before? How recently and how frequently? In evaluating downside risk, one has to consider just how the resume will read if you soon switch again.

I have heard the phrase, "Even if this move does not work out, it will certainly look good on my resume." I would *never* advise *against* taking a chance on a new industry or career solely because it might *not* look good on your resume, but in evaluating the pluses and minuses for changing, the above consideration is important enough to be seriously weighed.

By doing the above, you may come to the conclusion that you have job-hopped enough, and why make it any worse? On the other hand, you may conclude that you have never taken a chance—and there is no time like the present!

5 DIRECTORIES AND OTHER JOB MARKETING TOOLS

Whether you decide to look within your industry or outside, the actual job campaign will be similar. There are various tools you might use to accomplish your objective.

Within each industry there are various directories, trade associations, and membership lists. Within your own industry, you may already know what these materials are, or have them already. Outside of your industry prospecting can be made much easier with any of the following publications.

All of the following publications should be available at any decent sized library. If you happen to live in an area where they are not readily available, you may want to consider purchasing a couple of them. It is still a lot cheaper than paying several thousand dollars to an executive guidance firm.

1. *Thomas Register*, Thomas Publishing Company, One Penn Plaza, New York, N.Y., 10001. Breaks down all the manufacturers of every conceivable product category located within the United States. Also various cross indexes which give additional information, such as company size.

2. *Standard & Poor's Register of Corporations Directors and Executives*, Standard & Poor's Corporation, 345 Hudson Street, New York, N.Y., 10014. Lists all major companies and their management in the United States. Also includes information regarding size, location, and what businesses the companies are in. This directory includes a comprehensive list of management personnel and their titles.

3. *Dun's Million Dollar Directory*, Dun's Marketing Services. A Division of Dun & Bradstreet Inc., 3 Century Drive, Parsippany, New Jersey, 07054. Another directory listing all major companies and their management in the United States. Also includes information regarding size, location, and what industries the companies are in. The *Million Dollar Directory* has a particularly good breakdown by S.I.C. Code and Geographic Cross Index.

4. *Encyclopedia of Associations*, Gale Research Company, Book Tower, Detroit, Michigan, 48226. This publication provides exactly what the name implies, and could be extremely valuable. Just imagine, if you are interested in some exotic industry and you want to know what associations serve the industry, where are they, and how they can help you. It is all in the *Encyclopedia of Associations*.

5. *Guide to American Directories*, B. Klein Publications, P.O. BOX 8503, Coral Springs, Florida, 33065. How about that! So you want to know who all the "widget" companies are. Well, first find out if there is a directory serving the industry. If there is a directory serving any industry—chances are it will be listed in the above guide.

6. *State Directories of Manufacturers*. These are publications for each State containing the names of all manufacturers, distributors, and the products they produce and handle. These State Directories are invaluable because they locate various companies by products and towns. Because they only list companies within a particular State, they include many small companies which could be overlooked by the national directories. State directories also include information about each plant which is located within the State. They include the names of company management and addresses and telephone numbers.

Various State organizations publish their own directories. Frequently, they are published by the State Industrial Development Department, or the Chamber of Commerce.

Another source is, **Manufacturers' News, Inc., 3 East Huron Street, Chicago, Illinois 60611.** They distribute all the State Directories. They also handle several International Industrial Directories which could be a tremendous help if you are seeking to locate out of the Country.

7. *Encyclopedia of Business Information*, Gale Research Company, Book Tower, Detroit, Michigan, 48226. A detailed listing of sourcebooks, periodicals, organizations, directories, handbooks, bibliographies, and other sources of topical information. A very handy tool for someone in the job market.

8. *Standard Directory of Advertisers*, National Register Publishing Co., Inc., Skokie Illinois 60077. This publication breaks down all products and services and indicates the names of the companies, their product names, their officers, and contact information. Many of the marketing and advertising managers are also included, as well as the company's outside advertising agency.

9. *Ayer Directory of Publications and Periodicals*, Ayer Press 210 West Washington Square, Philadelphia, Pennsylvania 19106. This is basically a directory of all the newspapers and magazines published throughout the United States. The directory describes the types of publications and newspapers by the various markets they serve. It also includes an index as to where they are published and their circulation.

The Ayer Directory could be most helpful in determining where to look for appropriate classified ads.

10. A Valuable Source—*The Yellow Pages.* In fact, the Yellow Pages are just crammed with valuable information. By just thumbing through the Yellow Pages, you will come upon various industries and products which may be of interest. There are also cross references which could provide additional ideas.

Most libraries have the Yellow Pages from major cities all over the Country. If you are interested in a particular geographic area, just glance through the appropriate Yellow Pages. You can receive some valuable information about a city or town just by going through its Yellow Pages.

You can easily find out, by thumbing through the Yellow Pages, just what kind of businesses are in the area. Some other valuable information which can easily be found:

a. What kind of vital personal services are available, such as doctors, lawyers, accountants, etc.?

b. What kind and how many hospitals there are.

c. How many police and fire stations there are.

d. What kind of schools are available and how many.

e. Religious affiliations represented.

f. What kind of entertainment is listed.

g. How many restaurants and what kind.

h. How many libraries.

The above factors are most important in considering a move to a strange area.

You can also obtain copies of the Yellow Pages for different cities by requesting them from your local telephone company. Depending on which telephone company services your area, how many copies you request, and if you plan on making long distance calls to those areas—there may or may not be a service charge for the extra copies.

11. *Moody's Manuals*, Moody's Investors Service Inc., 99 Church Street, New York, N.Y., 10007. This is a continually updated financial service which describes what thousands of public companies are doing. Such information as a description of the company and its business, updated earnings, dividends, and pertinent business reports are continually coming out.

12. *Moody's Handbook of Common Stocks*, Moody's Investors Service Inc., 99 Church Street, New York, N.Y., 10007. Published by Moody's Investors Service, this quarterly publication has a fact sheet on thousands of publicly held companies.

13. *Standard Corporation Records*, Standard & Poor's Corporation, 345 Hudson Street, New York, N.Y., 10014. Publishes a financial service describing thousands of publicly held companies. Like Moody's, the publication is constantly updated for any pertinent developments affecting the listed companies.

14. *Standard & Poor's Stock Reports*, Standard & Poor's Corporation, 345 Hudson Street, New York, N.Y., 10014. This publication is categorized by companies listed on the New York Stock Exchange, American Stock Exchange, and the Over the Counter Markets. This service continually updates fact sheets describing information concerning publicly held companies.

15. *Value Line Investment Survey*, Arnold Bernhard & Company, 711 Third Avenue, New York, N.Y., 10017. Similar to Moody's, and Standard & Poor's, in many ways, but is different and unique enough in its approach to warrant recommendation. *Value Line* is also continually updating their company reports and analysis.

Moody's, Standard & Poor's, and *Value Line* all provide excellent financial services. Although there are similarities between publications, they are distinctive enough to warrant using all of them, if necessary, as cross references.

Each service might provide just one valuable piece of information about the company you are considering, which the others do not, to make cross referencing worthwhile.

16. *Subject Guide to Books in Print,* **R. R. Bowker Company (a Xerox Publishing Company), 1180 Avenue of the Americas, New York, N.Y. 10036.** As the title indicates, this publication lists every book which is in print. If one wanted to research a particular field to pursue, this book could be a valuable aid.

17. *Standard Periodical Directory,* **Oxbridge Communications, 1345 Avenue of the Americas, New York, N.Y. 10019.** Has valuable information on more than 60,000 periodicals.

18. *Readers Guide to Periodical Literature,* **H.W. Wilson Company, 950 University Avenue, Bronx, New York, N.Y. 10452.** This very valuable basic guide, which probably all of us have used at one time or another, lists all the subjects which have been written about in the various periodicals. Just about any subject pertaining to your job campaign can be researched by using this guide.

19. *Business Periodicals Index,* **H. W. Wilson Company, 950 University Avenue, Bronx, New York, N.Y. 10452.** Like the Readers Guide—except it focuses on business subjects.

20. *Business Information Sources,* **University of California Press, Berkeley and Los Angeles, California.** Basic annotated guide to selected business books and reference sources.

21. *Directory of Business and Financial Services,* **Special Libraries Association, 235 Park Avenue South, New York, N.Y. 10003.** This reference book deals with information services which are continually provided to assist with specific business needs.

6 RESUME MAILING CAMPAIGN

A. How Many Companies Should You Contact?

When companies are selected to be contacted, one should keep in mind that *probability will prevail.* Many executives do not realize, when they send their resumes out cold, that no matter how wonderfully it reads, the response will probably not be more than three or four percent. If you send out three to four hundred resumes, the probability is that you will not receive more than a dozen interview invitations. Out of those dozen interviews, you might receive three or four offers. Since we are dealing with probability, there are of course both exceptions and extremes.

The one very important point I want to stress on this subject is: *Do not become discouraged.* After sending out thirty or forty resumes and receiving only polite turn-down letters—*you have barely scratched the surface!*

Back in 1974, during the real estate crunch, a friend of mine lost his job as a sales manager for a major home builder. He was really bewildered. He had sent out nearly one hundred resumes without a "nibble." I might add that he had an excellent background and a very polished resume. What I said to him was, "Sending out resumes is a numbers game. You can draw a blank on the first hundred resumes, but you are liable to receive a half dozen interviews from the next one hundred."

I bet him a steak dinner that if he sent out four hundred more resumes, he would receive at least half a dozen offers. He followed my advice and sent out the additional four hundred resumes and received three attractive offers of which he chose one. So, he didn't get the additional three . . . you can only work on one job at a time anyway! I paid for the steaks, and today my friend is Vice President of that same firm he joined in 1974.

In fact, I can honestly state that I have never seen anyone who sent out several hundred well-prepared resumes who did not receive some offers. If the resumes are poorly prepared—then you may as well save the postage. Make the numbers work for you—not against you!

B. Do Not Forget the Cover Letter

Accompanying each resume should be a brief cover letter introducing yourself. The letter should request the reader to evaluate your credentials for an appropriate position within his organization. Make the letter brief and to the point. Nobody wants to read long cover letters. The letter should serve merely to break the ice and get the reader to continue through your resume.

Make sure that the letter quality matches the quality of the resume. There are few things worse than a cheap looking handwritten cover letter accompanying a professional-looking resume—except maybe a cheap-looking handwritten resume. . . .

A suggestion, when mailing out a large number of resumes, is to make a list of the individuals you are writing to, along with their

[YOUR LETTERHEAD]

August 4, 1979

Mr. John Doe, President *Faye Lockey*
Major Firm
Major Firm Plaza
Chicago, Illinois 60601

Dear Mr. Doe:

Enclosed is a copy of my resume for your review and evaluation. As you will note, I have a financial and accounting background. My professional career began fourteen years ago as a staff auditor with the XYZ Public Accounting Company and progressed to my present position as Division Controller for a $200 million dollar division of the RST Company.

My career interests aim towards the senior management areas of finance and accounting. Consideration for any appropriate career opportunities with your company would be greatly appreciated.

I hope to hear from you in the near future.

Thank you,
Sincerely,

[Signature]

Jim Applicant

Enclosure

company addresses. Once you complete the list you can easily avoid the drudgery of typing each letter individually. Bring your list of company names, addresses, and the individuals you are contacting to a professional secretarial service that has an automatic typewriter.

This is an electronic marvel that enables the typist to type each individual name, address, title, date, while the automatic typewriter types the body of the letter—by itself—in seconds. The completed letter gives the impression that it was individually typed for the reader.

This Sample Cover Letter would be aimed towards a senior financial or accounting management position. If the letter and resume was in answer to an ad or aimed towards a specific position, then you would indicate so in your career interests.

C.   Who Should Receive Your Letter and Resume?

This is a most critical aspect of your endeavor to switch employers. Sending your resume to the wrong individual in a company is like looking for water in the desert. The water probably will not be there—and neither will your potential job offer.

Always try to send your resume to the individual who you figure would be your *boss* if you are hired. If you are going after a Financial Vice President slot, then write to the Chairman or the President. You certainly would not want to write to the present Financial Vice President. Even if you do not indicate which position you are seeking, it does not take a genius to sense a threat, and the self preservation need sails your resume into the wastebasket. You can also receive a quick flip in the trash from someone too low on the totem pole.

If you are approaching a big company and you are not quite ready for top management, then do not make the common serious mistake of sending your resume to too high an executive. This is usually not a fatal mistake, but the President of a large company has things on his mind other than finding a junior or middle management slot for you. The resume is liable to sit on his, or his secretary's, desk until you are ready for top management! So, do not hold your breath waiting. . . .

What about the Personnel Department? When you send a resume cold to the personnel department, you are playing Russian roulette with your resume. If you are fortunate enough to send it to a high enough level within the Department and the Vice President of Personnel happens to spot it, then you might have a chance. Typically an underling will receive your resume and if, unfortunately, he does not happen to have a job requisition that fits your credentials—then into the file cabinet, or again the wastebasket.

Unfortunately, it has been my experience that personnel administrators have all they can do to accomplish their present work load, without going around trying to create positions. Like anything else, there are exceptions. During the years I have been an executive recruiter, I have encountered some truly outstanding personnel executives, who really would go out of their way if they spotted what they thought was talent described on that resume. In fact, I have seen cases where an astute Personnel Manager would plant the initial seed with top management when he ran across an exceptional resume—and before you knew it . . . a new employee was hired for a newly created position.

The potential immediate boss has the most to gain by your being hired. Lets face it, there is no one else within the company who would benefit more than your potential immediate supervisor. It's his workload that would be relieved, and he who stands to gain most directly if you do well—for if the employee does well, the boss looks good!

D. Following-Up The Resume

Once you have begun to mail out your resume, how long do you wait for a reply? When should you follow up? How should you follow up? These are all very important steps in the resume mailing process.

I usually recommend waiting about two weeks for a reply. If none has been received, then I recommend following-up with a telephone call. The groundwork has already been laid, and you have a perfect reason for calling—you want to know if they have received your resume and if there is any interest. This "one two punch" follow-up frequently gets "the squeaky wheel oiled." The mere fact that you followed up will sometimes prompt the resume recipient to invite you in for an interview—which is what you had hoped for in the first place. If you do not receive an interview invitation, then your phone call will have prompted a turn-down—which is what you would have received eventually anyway. Nobody wants to receive bad news, but in this case it is far better to receive it early than to have false hopes built up.

Make a tickler file card for each company you send a resume to. This way, you can systematically cross them off as you go. Also, date the card the day you mail the resume—so that if no reply is received, you know when to follow up.

E. Personal and Confidential

To increase the odds of your letter and resume actually being read by the prospective employer, type "Personal and Confidential" on the envelope of all resumes and cover letters that you mail out.

Secretaries will think twice about even opening it—never mind tossing it into the wastebasket!

7 TELEPHONE CAMPAIGN

This is an approach which is so effective . . . and yet so few individual job seekers use it. Where else can you interrupt a conversation and obtain immediate response? If we ever did in person what the telephone does, we would be considered extremely rude. Yet, when that telephone rings, we drop everything and answer it.

An effective telephone campaign should be used simultaneously with your resume campaign. Select certain companies to which you will send your resume, and others which you will call. Any system for dividing those to call and those to write that you are comfortable with is fine. Use the same research materials and appropriate names as you will in your resume mailings, only for different companies.

Keep in mind, though, that there is an advantage to calling the local companies as opposed to the long distance ones. One obvious advantage is the savings in your telephone bill.

If your company is aware that you are leaving, they may provide you with a desk, phone, and perhaps even access to the WATS line. In fact, a telephone campaign almost has to be done when you are either on vacation, have left your present employer, or when they know you are looking. How else would you have time to make the calls unless you worked a second or third shift.

A second reason for concentrating, if at all possible, your telephone campaign locally is that when you call an employer long distance, chances are the best you can hope for is that he requests your resume and gets back to you. There are occasions when, if you happen to hit the employer at the right time with the right pitch, he may just tell you to hop on a plane for an interview. The latter is the exception though, when long distances are involved.

When you telephone a company within a reasonable driving distance, your goal should be for your contact to invite you directly in for an interview. Some may still request a resume, even though they are interested, but the majority of employers should set up an interview.

A. How To Get Through To The Decision Maker

Remember, when selecting who to call, choose the one who can hire you and will benefit the most—as we discussed earlier in the resume campaign.

When the secretary answers, your conversation might go like this, "Hello, John Doe please." Avoid asking for "Mr. Doe." This will only suggest that you do not know Mr. Doe. You want to avoid, if at all possible, the third degree from John Doe's secretary. If she senses that you know him, she may put you through without any further questions. You want to come across as sincere, and with a controlled confidence, but yet not too informal or presumptuous.

If she asks you more than your name, it may sound like this:

64

"What is this in reference to?" You answer, "This is a personal call." Nine times out of ten the personal call approach will work. Secretaries are hesitant about meddling in their boss's personal affairs.

If she does not put you through at this point, she will usually respond with "Does Mr. Doe know you?" What you answer here and how you answer is extremely delicate. One answer might be "yes" and pray that she accepts it and puts you through. She is also liable to tell her boss that you know him, and in that case when asked by the boss, "Did you tell my secretary that you knew me?" you might just answer "because my call is of a personal and confidential nature, and she was so efficiently screening me [it does not hurt to lightly compliment the boss's secretary] I thought it would be easier to say I know you."

When asked, "will Mr. Doe know who you are?" by the secretary, you might answer simply, "No." Be firm and confident when answering "No." If she then asks "May I tell Mr. Doe what this call is in reference to?" Your answer might be, "I'm sorry, but it is a personal matter." This is the second time you have told her that your call is of a personal nature. By this time she should put you through to the boss. If she comes back with something like "I am sorry, but I screen all of Mr. Doe's calls." Do not fight it—life is too short. . . .

Explain to her that you are employed with a competitor in a key position, and you heard that her boss is expanding the department and may be interested in hiring someone with your type of background. Now there might be a good chance that the boss is thinking about hiring an additional member for his department. Your call just may fertilize the idea. He has not got around to writing up a job requisition yet, but having a qualified candidate call him from a competitor may be all he needs to get the ball rolling. He will definitely at least talk to you.

Even if he was not thinking about hiring any additional help, the mere fact that his secretary tells him that you heard they were expanding should prompt him to talk to you. It is a good, positive subject and everyone enjoys talking about pleasant subjects.

65

If the boss is unavailable, or out of his office, have him return your call either at home or on a private line. You may even consider hiring an answering service to receive your messages during your job campaign. Answering services can be hired for short term periods and are usually most reasonable in price, especially when you consider the positive results which can be gained by using them.

If you are with a competitor, he may feel uncomfortable having a confidential conversation with you once your switchboard operator answers as his friendly competitor. You want him as comfortable and relaxed as possible. If you do not have a private line, an answering service, or someone at home to take the message—leave word that you will call back.

B. Selling Yourself to the Decision Maker

You might say something like this: "Hello, John Doe, my name is Jim Smith [refer to the boss as 'Mr. Doe' if you know him to be significantly older than you], and I am presently employed as a plant manager [assuming you are a plant manager] with another company in your industry. I understand that your company is expanding, and may have some opportunities for candidates with my background." As mentioned previously, you just might be motivating him to do a little expanding. Every executive likes to feel that his company *is* expanding—so if he says "We are not," then take his word for it. If he answers "Yes, we are, and we are always looking for well-qualified candidates" then you might ask him specifically "what backgrounds in particular are you looking for?" He may reply with a specific job description or just general backgrounds. In any event, you have him talking to you about his needs and plans.

After you feel that the prospective boss has given you some clues as to his department needs—then you might describe your background and why it might fit what he is looking for.

If the prospective boss asks on the telephone "Why are you looking?" be very positive in your answer. Do not say "I am looking because I hate my boss and my crummy job." Although you may feel that way, you must be positive. Indicate to the prospective boss that you are not really looking, but you thought there might be some excellent opportunities with his company due to the planned expansion you heard about. You are simply giving his company an opportunity to consider you for their future plans without making any specific commitments.

If you sense that he is interested in your background, then suggest that the two of you meet for a confidential preliminary discussion. He may beat you to the punch and request it first, but if he does not—don't be bashful. As everyone knows in the field of sales, if you do not ask for the order—you will not get the sale.

If he states that his personnel department does all the hiring, ask him if he has submitted a recent job requisition to them. If the answer is "no" then go on to your next call. But first ask him if he knows of any appropriate leads for you to explore, considering your background.

Quite frequently, an employer will turn you down, but provide a lead that strikes *"pay dirt."*

If the answer is "yes" ask him for the name of the appropriate individual in personnel to talk to. Also ask if you may use his name. This is very important, because if you call the Personnel Manager cold, you may get nowhere, but if you indicate that "John Doe, the Vice President asked that I call you about setting up an interview"—you practically have your foot in the door.

A word of caution: If nothing further is expected from this contact, do not forget to emphasize that your company is unaware that you would even consider another opportunity, and therefore you would appreciate it if he would keep your conversation extremely confidential.

Again, there is an element of risk, but in order to make gains, sometimes we have to take calculated risks.

Even if there is interest on the part of the prospective boss, it does not hurt to emphasize the confidentiality of the matter. By doing this, you are also telling him that you are still gainfully employed . . . nothing wrong with that.

C. Cover a Lot of Territory in a Short Period

Many companies are just beginning to realize how efficient the telephone can be. There have been numerous cost studies indicating that the telephone is an extremely economical tool for companies to use. Where a salesman would make ten in-person calls per day—by using the telephone to prospect, he could make forty to fifty calls per day. Many salesmen qualify prospects on the telephone and then set up the appointments. This obviously saves a lot of time.

Admittedly, there are some products and services which lend themselves to cold telephone calling much better than others. *Searching for a job is one example of selling which certainly lends itself to the telephone.*

Think of the employment agency industry—they use the telephone successfully all day long. They call employers cold and pitch applicants. In your case, you would be pitching yourself—which should be a lot easier. Nobody knows your own qualifications as you do. At least, the employer knows there is no fee attached. . . .

The executive search industry uses the telephone extensively to recruit candidates. I would estimate that over ninety-five percent of all candidates recruited are initially approached on the telephone. I personally make an average of over forty recruiting calls per day. In addition there are the incoming calls.

Do as the professionals do and take advantage of the telephone.

8 ANSWERING THE JOB ADS

Outside of contacting companies cold, this is the second most valuable source for leads. There is both a distinct advantage and disadvantage to job ads in newspapers and other publications. The distinct advantage is that if there is an ad, then you usually have a bonafide job opening. An exception would be when a company simply wants to see just what or who is available out in the marketplace. They run an ad and hope that employees of their competition will respond for some subtle interrogation, and nothing more. These companies also have to be careful because this game can be played two ways. Competitors will sometimes send employees over for interviews on what is referred to in the trade as "search and destroy missions," or "fishing expeditions."

Another exception is when a company wants to promote one of their own employees to fill the position, but before they do, they just want to see how he measures up against some outside competition. It usually is an exercise in futility for the outside candidates.

This situation will happen more frequently when a "blind ad" is used. They obviously do not want the internal candidate to know that he is not the overwhelming favorite.

This is also a good reason to be very selective in responding to "blind ads." It may be your own company placing the ad—for whatever reasons they may have. The vast majority of job ads are quite legitimate, but like anything else . . . let good judgement and common sense prevail.

The distinct disadvantage I mentioned in the first paragraph is the competition the job ad will attract. There could literally be hundreds of responses to a particular ad. Figure the odds: If you are only competing against the resume reader liking your background or needing your background—that is one thing. If you are one of two hundred responses, then you, as the fish, are now swimming in a bigger pond. . . .

Incidentally, if you answer an identified job ad and receive no response—then also follow up in about two weeks. Whether you send a resume cold or respond to an ad—follow-up is a must for the same basic reasons.

I might also suggest the following when turned down in response to an identified job ad. If the resume was sent to the Personnel Department per ad instructions and they turned you down—either by letter or after you followed up with a phone call—then do not be afraid to go one step further. This suggestion is particularly encouraged when you suspect that there was a large ad response, but honestly feel that the advertised position was just made for you.

The Personnel Department is frequently told by the department head seeking to fill the opening to, "Select the best three candidates and pass them on." It does not take a vivid imagination to conclude that with a great number of responses, your resume could literally get lost in the shuffle—or at least only receive a superficial appraisal. Another factor could be an honest difference of opinion between the Personnel Manager and the department head. If the department head had seen your resume, you might have been selected!

I have company clients who hire by committee. It is sometimes literally like a "fraternity rush." If there is a committee of five, then you have five appraisals and frequently there is a great disparity among them. Your career is obviously too important to take the chance that the Personnel Manager made an honest mistake in turning you down.

After being turned down by the Personnel Department, you have absolutely nothing to lose by contacting the department head by telephone and indicating that you were turned down but feel you warrant further consideration—then proceeding to honestly and sincerely give your reasons why. Make sure you do not knock whoever turned you down. You want to create a positive impression on the department head and the easiest way to "blow it" is to sing the "sour grapes tune." Keep in mind that the object of this call is to communicate to the department head the benefits of his hiring you.

After you have completed your presentation, one of three things will most likely happen:

1. The department head will not be sold, and will immediately confirm the Personnel Department's decision to turn you down.

2. He will offer encouragement and indicate that he wants to discuss this matter further with the Personnel Department. At least you will have the satisfaction of knowing that the department head now knows who you are, and he himself partook in the decision-making process—if you are turned down.

3. He thinks you are a "gutsy" person. He likes "gutsy" people and proceeds to invite you in for an interview.

You had nothing to lose and everything to gain by going the one step further.

If you are utilizing the job ads in newspapers, and you would really like to relocate out of town, simply subscribe to the local newspaper which serves your desired locale. It is very inexpensive to have an out-of-town newspaper mailed to you for a period of a few months. Since Sunday Editions frequently carry the most job want ads—you can simply subscribe to the Sunday Edition and your cost is significantly reduced.

When evaluating which newspaper to subscribe to in a distant city, make sure that you do not waste your money subscribing to the number two newspaper in terms of quantity and quality of ads.

If nothing else, ask the supervisor in the circulation department if his newspaper has the most job want ads for the market they serve, and if not, which paper does? Also ask what kind of job ads they typically run. Many of the major newspapers have a Sunday display section which feature management and professional positions.

I have found that one of the best sources of professional and management job listings is *The Wall Street Journal.* Not only does this paper continually carry a substantial cross-section of different kinds of professional and management positions from all over, but breaks down their publication into Regional Editions. If you live in Chicago, but want to relocate to California, you can easily subscribe to the Western Edition of *The Wall Street Journal* on a temporary basis. The advantage of subscribing to a particular Regional Edition of *The Wall Street Journal* would be the overwhelming preponderance of openings being advertised located in your desired part of the country.

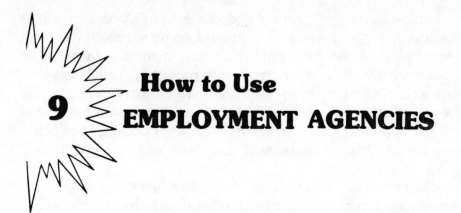

How to Use
9 EMPLOYMENT AGENCIES

The term "Employment Agency" is an all encompassing description of an industry that at one extreme might be placing the unskilled, all the way up to the other, recruiting top management in the six figure income level. The question "what is the difference between an employment agency and an executive search firm?" might be answered as follows: "In many cases there is none." In other cases the differences are tremendous! The key is the kind of employment agency we are referring to, and the way they are being utilized.

Employment agencies frequently charge the individual a fee. This is done when the agency cannot convince the employer to pay the fee. On the other hand, many employment agencies that deal only with management and professional personnel do not charge fees to individuals. They simply will not accept a job order unless the fee is paid by the company.

In most states, employment agencies are regulated, required to be licensed, and frequently bonded. Executive search firms are pretty well exempt from state regulation in most instances. The reason for this is that the states want to protect the individuals who use employment agencies from being taken advantage of. This becomes especially obvious when employment agencies charge fees to applicants for positions. In lower level positions this is frequently the case, the applicant in many instances, pays his own fee.

What many states have done is basically differentiate between an employment agency and an executive search firm by the salary level of positions they can handle, and by who compensates them. An example might be in a particular state where executive search firms are not allowed to place anyone in a position which will pay a salary of less than $15,000 per year. Also, executive search firms must work for the company client and be entirely compensated by the company client.

If an employment agency places lower level personnel, then they obviously have to be fully licensed by the state. Employment agencies which function at much higher levels will also frequently remain licensed employment agencies, rather than executive search firms, so that they can occasionally place and recruit management trainees to accommodate their company clients. It can be irritating to an employer when a firm can recruit the Sales Manager, but is unable to help staff the sales *force!*

Another reason why a firm might rather be a licensed employment agency is when the economy gets bad. It can sometimes become quite challenging to convince companies to pay substantial fees for recruiting candidates when other companies are laying off at a fast rate. Those are times when unsolicited resumes arrive in droves, and many of those candidates would gladly pay a fee to get a job.

Not only are employment agencies licensed in many states, but so are the counsellors they employ. Several states now give an examination to the individual applying for a counsellor's license before one is granted. Many states have done a pretty decent job in trying to upgrade the industry.

Even the National Employment Association, the trade association for the employment agency industry, has tried to enhance their image by issuing a certificate of achievement to counsellors who have passed a comprehensive examination on their profession.

Even with all the attempts to upgrade the employment agency industry, there remains constant problems. Any time you have an industry which is compensated by commissions there are going to be overzealous participants trying to make a "fast buck." The same could also be said of the securities industry, the real estate industry, the insurance industry, etc. Over the years, I have seen participants in the employment agency industry, and executive search business, run the gamut from total incompetence to extremely competent and professional.

There is quite a rivalry between employment agencies specializing in the executive job market, and executive search firms. As I indicated earlier, there is frequently no difference whether a company hires an employment agency or an executive search firm to conduct a search. When the employment agency is actually going to recruit candidates to fill the job, the employment agency is functioning exactly as an executive search firm—they are not merely waiting for candidates to walk through their door.

Executive search firms will sometimes employ self-preservation tactics and refer to employment agencies as really serving the lower level job market—as many agencies do. They also refer to employment agencies as not being recruiters, but rather merely waiting for applicants to come to them—and in many instances this is true.

What irks the executive recruiters are employment agencies which function exactly like executive recruiters and yet still have the licence flexibility to make a job campaign for a promising candidate *or* place a lower level applicant.

Whereas an executive search firm works solely for the client company, an employment agency can work for either the company or the individual. Even though the agency might be compensated by whoever hires you, they can still run a job search campaign on your behalf. Specifically, employment agencies specializing in professional and management personnel will frequently run a job search campaign for you—approaching only those companies who will pay the entire employment agency fee. In this day and age, unless the economy is really down, most companies will gladly (well, maybe not quite *gladly*) pay an employment agency fee to hire good people.

If you are an especially outstanding candidate, then it behooves the employment agency to make a job search campaign in your behalf. There is nothing like an outstanding applicant to "break the ice" with an employer. The theory is that the employer will assume that since this candidate being presented is pretty good, then the agency must also be pretty good. Sometimes yes, and sometimes no.

An employment agency or search firm is only as good as the candidates they deal with. If an individual recruited or placed with a company turns out to be a poor employee, then it is guilt by association—the firm that placed him could not be much better. If the placement is highly successful, then there is a high probability that the employer will return with more search assignments. This is an obvious long-range motivation for employment agencies and search firms.

A. One Distinct Advantage in Using an Employment Agency

The distinct advantage in your using an employment agency is that they can help you in preparing for your interviews. The employment counsellor, if he is worth anything, should possess some insight into the company and perhaps even into the personalities of the individuals who will make the ultimate hiring decision. If there are any peculiarities about the employer or other pertinent information which could increase your chances for a successful interview—the intermediaries are in a position to help you. If your employment counsellor does not possess the necessary insight to help you, then he is at least in a position to obtain it.

Search firms can also offer you valuable insight, but you will most likely be dealing with them when *they* choose, not *you*.

If other candidates have also been sent to the employer by the agency, and have been turned down, try to find out why. What is the so-called "hot button" for this particular employer? What are his particular likes or dislikes? What salary level do they really want to pay? How much was the last employee who held the position earning?

I heard of an employment counsellor, some years ago, who was trying to place a costume jewelry salesman with one of his client companies. He must have sent his client half-a-dozen tall, handsome, athletic-looking salesmen. They all fitted the image of what an "All-American Salesman" ought to look like—whatever that may be. All of them had related product sales experience. After having all of them turned down, the employment counsellor still could not figure out just what was the matter. The employers indicated that they were all fine young men, but they were not quite what they were looking for. Finally the employment counsellor arranged to visit the company and meet the owners. The company was owned and operated by three brothers—all of whom were under five feet five, and weighed in excess of 200 lbs. They were also bald. There were also three other salesmen employed with the company who were carbon copies of the three brothers.

Within a few days the counsellor, with new-found wisdom, sent over to the employer a nice, young, short, and portly salesman whose background was selling automotive supplies. He was made an offer and subsequently hired. The counsellor had finally come up with a "round peg" for a "round hole."

B. Choose Your Own Employment Counsellor

When arriving at the employment agency to register, do not be afraid to ask for the manager of the agency first, and explain to him what your experience and background are. Request a senior counsellor. If the manager feels that you are readily marketable, then he should happily accommodate you. If he does not, and gives you a hard time; politely thank him for his time and be on your way. Your career and your time are too important to risk with some incompetent counsellor—who started the day before, and probably will not be there the following week when you call to follow-up on why nothing positive has been accomplished.

If you really impress the manager he may try to hire you to work in the employment agency as an employment counsellor. I would estimate that over ninety percent of the employment counsellors are hired from the ranks of individuals coming to the employment agency looking for a job. Most employment agencies pay their counsellors primarily a commission except for a small draw—so they are almost always anxious to hire another one.

When you select an agency and a counsellor, do not give him the impression that you are registered, or will be registered, with several other employment agencies. If you are fortunate enough to draw a top counsellor to work with, then you can be sure he did not become that way by trying to place applicants who were registered with a dozen different agencies. If you are impressed with the counsellor, tell him you will use him exclusively. You may even really do that.

There are some very talented and creative employment counsellors who can really do some good for you if they are properly motivated. It is no surprise that the most competent employment counsellors make the most money, and some earn quite substantial incomes for themselves.

Since you will not really know just how good the counsellor is until he produces, under no circumstances should you give up on your own job search campaign. Even if you are convinced that he will arrange more good, solid interviews than you can handle. Unfortunately, it is "the nature of the beast" for the counsellor to convince the applicant that he should rely exclusively on him for the best interviews, and not go to any other employment agency. Only time will tell. . . .

C. Employment Agency Contracts

There are many different contracts used in the industry, but I have never seen one yet which I felt was worth signing. Many of them have clauses which obligate you for a substantial portion of the fee if you accept a job, even though you then change your mind, and do not spend one day on the job. Others obligate you for the fee if you spend a short period on the job, then leave; no matter whether the position was fee-paid by the employer or not. If you sign an employment agency contract, then leave your job in less time than the agency guaranteed you for, you will probably be obligated to the agency for whatever they have to refund to the employer.

Each state has different laws governing employment agency contracts with job applicants, and the obligation could range from nothing—all the way up to the entire fee. In many states, the reason for your leaving your job within the "guarantee period" makes a substantial difference to your level of obligation under a signed employment agency contract. If you never want to pay an employment agency fee, then simply never sign an employment agency contract. Specify that you only want to be considered for fee-paid jobs where you have no obligation whatsoever to the employment agency.

In fairness to those employment agencies that have made it a policy not to work with any applicant who does not sign their contract, I suggest you at least show it to an attorney before signing. There are some employment agencies wanting to insure that *someone* is going to compensate them if they successfully place you. Because employment agencies typically work with companies on an oral contract basis, there have been cases of misunderstanding between the employer and the agency as to who will pay the fee. By having your signature on the dotted line of a contract, the employment agency has obtained an insurance policy which provides payment from you if the company refuses to pay the fee.

If you *do* sign a contract, so that the agency will work with you, but do not want to pay a fee, then indicate emphatically that you will only accept interviews for fee-paid positions.

It is not unheard of for an employment counsellor to send an applicant who has indicated that he will not pay a fee, but who signed the contract, for an interview with an employer knowing full-well that the employer expects the fee to be paid by the applicant. What the counsellor hopes to accomplish is one of two goals:

1.   The employers will become so infatuated with the applicant that they change their mind and pay the fee. Meanwhile, the counsellor will try to coax the employer into paying by casually mentioning another excellent company who would be more than willing to pay the fee for such a qualified applicant. An employment agency would almost always prefer to have the commitment to pay the fee come from the company. Typically, an oral contract from a solvent company is more assuring to an employment agency than an individual's signed contract.

2.   The applicant falls in love with the job and the company, and agrees to pay the fee rather than pass up the opportunity of a lifetime.

While on the interview, when you have signed a contract, always confirm with the employer who is paying the fee in the event they hire you. You should confirm with the employer who is paying the fee even when you have *not* signed an employment agency contract. Why take any chances on a misunderstanding? A confirmation during the first interview can save a lot of grief when you are about to accept an offer.

Many of the employment agencies that aim at the management and professional positions have simply done away with contracts. They only deal with companies that pay the fee, so the subject of contracts with individual applicants is not germane.

At the management and professional levels, companies pay the employment agency fee the great majority of the time. Good people are hard to find, and it is frequently more efficient for a company to use an employment agency, or executive search firm, than to waste a lot of time and money trying to hire someone themselves.

D.   Do Not Discuss Which Other Companies You Are Talking To

One of the most fruitful methods of obtaining job order leads is to question the applicant about where else he has been or is going. It is amazing how many applicants will just "run-off at the mouth" that they are under consideration here, there, and everywhere. Each company mentioned, becomes an invitation for the employment counsellor to try and knock you out of the running by recommending a candidate of his own. As soon as you have completed boosting your ego and have left the office, you can bet that the counsellor will be on the telephone to your best lead—with a candidate he feels is better than you!

A little game that counsellors play is to ask you, "So that we do not cross wires, which other companies are you talking to?" Tell the employment counsellor, "I have just started my job search campaign and have only talked to a couple of companies that I am sure you would not be approaching." This should tip him off that if he is going to make any money on you . . . it will be from placing you—and not living off your leads!

E.   Employment Agency Application Form—Reference Line

Most employment agencies use their own standard job application forms which ask for references. If you do fill them out, make sure that you write: "<u>CONFIDENTIAL DO NOT CONTACT WITHOUT PERMISSION</u>" right above the references. Generally, I would recommend that, instead of listing references on the application, you write: "<u>CONFIDENTIAL—REFERENCES FURNISHED UPON REQUEST</u>." Make it very clear to the counsellor that you do not want anyone at your present or past employers contacted without your permission. You are gainfully employed and want to remain that way!

In hunting for job orders, counsellors are sometimes anxious to check particular references just as an excuse to call the company. You do not need that kind of reference check!

F. Discussing a Bad Experience

If you are utilizing the services of an employment agency, executive search firm, or any other personnel consultant, and you are unfortunate enough to discuss a job from which you were fired, how might you handle this delicate situation? Few individuals care to discuss their dismissal from a job. In fact, if they must they almost always find some reason for being fired which makes them feel better. In creating a fictitious reason for being fired from a job, the candidate frequently fails to use empathy in thinking out just how his fabrication will appear to the interviewer. In all my years as both an employment counsellor and executive recruiter, I have never had anyone tell me that the reason he or she got fired was for doing a lousy job. . . .

In many cases, it is really quite important that you do discuss this matter before you are presented to the employer. There are several practical ways of discussing an unpleasant present or prior job experience. A preliminary discussion of the bad experience you have had with a past job can help prepare you for actually meeting the prospective employer.

If you were fired from a recent job because you did a lousy job—there still had to be underlying reasons for it. Maybe you were too lenient with your subordinates and let them take advantage of you. Maybe you did not delegate responsibility, and attempted to do everything yourself. Maybe you just did not have the right background or training, and now you have taken steps to correct the situation. Maybe you had personal or health problems which have been corrected.

You want to give positive, common sense reasons why it did not work, and why you are confident that you have learned from your mistakes and are a better person for it.

I do not believe in dwelling on negative points, but it is far better for *you* to bring them up when they are going to present themselves anyways, either with the intermediary or the employer.

Depending on just what the negative point is in your background, and supposing you are not sure how to handle it, discussing things first with an executive recruiter, employment counsellor, or guidance counsellor can be of significant help. Remember, though, who is paying them, and gauge the magnitude of the blemish on your resume, when deciding how to handle this situation.

There is a calculated risk when you confess something pretty bad in your background to an executive recruiter or employment counsellor. You may ruin your chances of ever being recommended.

On the other hand, something that you were previously fired for might not seem that significant to the recruiter or counsellor. Without being disloyal to their company client, they may make some suggestions to you as to how you might handle this delicate subject.

G. Checking Out The Employment Agency or Search Firm

If you are going to deal with an employment agency or executive search firm on a personal basis, find out all you can about them. The easiest way to do this is to ask them straight questions, and draw your own conclusions. Do not be afraid to inquire at what salary levels they do most of their work. Ask the counsellor or recruiter, "How long have you, personally, been in the business?" What are some of the positions they have filled, and for whom? How long has the firm been in business?

Also, I suggest that if you are serious about using any particular firm, you "place the shoe on the other foot" and request references from both the firm and the individual counsellor or recruiter you will be dealing with. Your career is just too important not to take these precautions.

Any search firm or employment agency which will not produce good references *should not be used.*

When evaluating an employment agency, think of anyone you know or have heard about who may have had dealings with them. Ask them, straight out, what they thought—both the positive and negative. You might be surprised by what people will tell you about their own experiences. A few calls to friends could save a tremendous amount of time wasting and aggravation.

On the surface, it is very difficult to judge whether an agency or search firm is any good. Again, your successful dealings with search firms will probably come when *they approach you*—so this is really aimed at selecting a good employment agency.

Some large national chains are very good, while other large organizations are pretty bad. Some small ones are totally incompetent, while others are truly outstanding. Each firm, large or small, has to be evaluated and checked out individually. More specifically, each counsellor within each firm you will be dealing with has to be individually judged. The firm is only as good as the counsellor assigned to you!

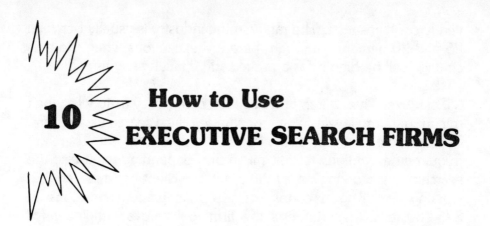

How to Use
EXECUTIVE SEARCH FIRMS

10

Executive recruiters are frequently referred to as "headhunters" or "bodysnatchers." I guess a fair definition of an executive search firm would be: "Any organization which is engaged in the business of seeking out, identifying, appraising, and recommending potential executives for their corporate clients." The client could also be other than a profit-making corporation, such as an association or a government agency. The executive search firm is compensated solely by the corporation—not the individual. In many instances the executive search firm is paid a retainer by the client; although frequently they will search out candidates on an exclusive contingency basis. It all depends on the relationship between the executive search firm and the client. If there is a long and active association between the search firm and the client, then the search firm will not be as concerned about being sent out on a "wild goose chase" and not getting paid. While some executive search firms work solely on an hourly rate, most receive a percentage of the yearly compensation. The range in the industry is usually between 25 and 30 percent, although there are exceptions when the percentage will be higher for a particularly difficult assignment.

Each executive search firm has their own policy as to what their minimum salary level is when they undertake a search assignment. Typically, the minimum salary is around $25,000 a year. There are frequently exceptions to that minimum, depending what else the search firm is working on for the client. If a client has a search firm working on filling a couple of top management positions at $75,000, and then requests the firm to locate an engineer for $20,000—you can be sure that common sense and good judgement will prevail.

There are literally thousands of executive search firms across the U.S., and each one has their own specialty and method of operation. Most executive search firms service all job functions in all industries. This not only creates more variety in their own daily routine, but enables a search firm to service every department within their client company. The only basic criterion is that the position is high enough up the corporate ladder to warrant the minimum salary level for which they will accept a search assignment.

Some executive search firms specialize in one or two industries, while others specialize in particular job categories such as accountants, lawyers, engineers, salesmen.

When looking for executive search firms to send your resume to, try to remember that they are concerned with filling job openings for their client companies. The executive recruiter is not interested in trying to find you a job. He only makes money on your resume when it just happens to fit one of his search assignments. Unlike other professions, most of the time the executive recruiter does *not* want to talk to you. He cannot charge you for his time so he typically would just as soon you mailed in your resume without any personal contact. If he wants you—he will call you!

Individuals frequently call up executive search firms to make an appointment for a personal interview, and then are disappointed when the well-trained receptionist will not accommodate them. If executive search firms saw *everyone* who requested an interview, then they just could not function. Also, unless your credentials are outstanding, do not expect any more from the executive search firm than a polite form letter indicating that they will keep your resume on file for the future.

When a company hires an executive search firm, they usually set their standards a notch higher than if they looked on their own. Companies feel, and rightfully so, that if they are going to pay a substantial fee to an executive search firm, then they want to hire the best candidates available. Employers feel that they could easily hire the *average* job seeker on their own. They expect the recruiters to do just that . . . recruit! That means going out and returning with the *ideal* candidate who was not in the job market and who never would have responded to a newspaper ad. You might say that the "headhunter" is really looking for whoever is *not* looking for him!

The executive recruiter's role is to contact a theoretically happy employee of a rival company, and try to get him frustrated. If he appears satisfied, the recruiter has to make him suddenly dissatisfied by creating a picture of a much better opportunity.

One of the most common "games" that executive "headhunters" play is one where they call an executive and ask him if he might recommend someone for a very important search assignment the recruiter is trying to fill. (When they put food on the table, all jobs have a tendency to become "very important.") The recruiter continues to infer that, since the executive is *eminently qualified,* he would be a good individual to recommend some candidates. After a few minutes of such a standard conversation, it should become apparent to the executive that the recruiter is really trying to recruit *him.* What the recruiter is really hoping when he asks, "Can you recommend anyone?" is that the voice on the other end will answer "Yes—me!"

I suppose this is a rather blunt way of putting it, but individuals who are so anxious to find out *who and where the executive recruiters are*—could more wisely spend their time searching out potential employers and then contacting them directly!

When your telephone rings at the office, and the voice at the other end of the line identifies himself as an executive recruiter, he might say something like this: "John Doe? My name is Bruce Moses, and I am an executive recruiter with a firm called Pro-Search, here in Chicago. The reason I am calling is that you were mentioned, in confidence, as perhaps having the background for which I am looking for one of our corporate clients. Can you speak freely?" After you return to earth from being up in cloud nine— there are some very specific things you should do:

1. *Determine if you really can speak freely.* Do not be so anxious as to risk someone overhearing your conversation. If you determine that you cannot speak freely—then get his telephone number and call him back later, or arrange to talk to him in the evening.

2. *If you can speak freely,* confirm that the recruiter is really who he says he is. Take his number, and call him back. Also, before calling him back, confirm his identity with the Yellow Pages or telephone operator. This is just a minor precaution, that maybe one candidate in fifty actually bothers with. The recruiter will ask you a lot of personal information on the phone, so by all means know he really is who he represents to be.

He should not be offended by your confirming his identity. If he is—then immediately end the conversation, and consider yourself lucky that you did not disclose any information. . . .

3. Ask the voice at the other end of the line *what exactly he is looking for*—where the position is located—and what is the salary range. You may save both of you a lot of time by asking the recruiter a few preliminary questions. Why let him question you for an hour, only to find out that the job pays less than you are currently earning, and is located in some area you would not consider in a million years? That is, unless you desperately need a job.

If, after talking, there is mutual interest, then the recruiter will either request a resume or indicate that he will soon be back to you, or both.

If you do decide to submit a resume, keep in mind the position for which you are being considered. Do not mail in a resume that is aimed at something entirely different. If you are going to consider what the executive "headhunter" has to offer, then do it right and prepare a new resume just for him—if necessary.

Sending an outdated resume to the recruiter, or showing up for an interview with one, is just using poor judgement. Unfortunately, I have received resumes from candidates I have recruited with the most recent experience written in longhand—and the rest type-written. What that candidate has done, without realizing it, is *diminish* the most recent few years of experience. A reader will tend to skim quickly over the longhand and go directly into the type-written portion. At least the above candidates filled in their most recent experience. Many candidates have shown up for interviews with just an outdated resume. An outdated resume which leaves out, for example, the last three or four years entirely . . . and is really much worse than no resume at all! Here you have downplayed what should be your most valuable three or four years of job experience. You may have good intentions of explaining your omitted few years verbally to the interviewer, but he will probably just forget, or if he takes some notes not get everything.

It would be better either to wait to submit your resume, or to arrive with no resume and then prepare it later—just for that employer. If there was not much time between the initial contact and the actual interview, then any interviewer should empathize with that situation.

Keep in mind that you will probably be one of many candidates under consideration. If a "headhunter" tells you that you are the only one they are talking to—then that is a red flag for you to end the conversation. Executive recruiters do not consider just one candidate at a time for their client. I have had search assignments where I actually talked to hundreds of candidates.

If the recruiter indicates that he is going to recommend three to five candidates, which is fairly common, try to have yourself scheduled either last, or close to it. The theory here is that when it comes time for the final decision, you will be the most easily remembered—especially if the interviewing process really drags out.

Frequently, a recruiter or employment counsellor may schedule one or two weak candidates in the beginning, just to make the best ones appear even better. Try to get the best position. If the recruiter absolutely insists that you lead off the pack, then I would say your chances are quite slim of ever receiving an offer. You are the "loss leader." You can bet that this "headhunter" has the "heavy-hitters" following you.

Be leery of the "headhunter" who says he is interested in *you*, but proceeds to ask questions about your employer's table of organization and who else does what. You may have been the easiest person for him to get hold of, and all he really is doing is "casing the joint" for his real target. Unfortunately, "fishing expeditions" on the part of both the candidate and the executive recruiter are more common than I would like to admit.

If there is an obvious mismatch determined by both the candidate and the recruiter, the recruiter will invariably ask you who else you know who might fit what he is looking for. *Under no circumstances* should you ever recommend fellow employees—unless they are close friends who have taken you into their confidence concerning their own job search—or there is someone in the company who you would like to see working some place else. . . .

An example might be a rival executive with whom you are competing for a promotion, or a boss who is "a real pain." If you ever recommend anyone else who works for the same employer, make absolutely sure that you confirm with the recruiter that he is sworn to secrecy as to where he received his lead. When you think about it, it is really disloyal for an employee to recommend another employee to an executive recruiter. After all, his employer is putting bread on his table, so he should not give out names just to impress the "executive headhunter." Incidentally, the "headhunter" may be quite pleased to receive the names, but he is certainly *not* going to be favorably impressed with you. You have demonstrated a disloyalty to your employer which could be a strike against you for future consideration.

Recommending to a recruiter candidates who are employed with other companies is fine—and is not a bad way to make a friend of the executive recruiter. You do him an ethical favor, and he just might remember you the next time he has an appropriate opening.

Occasionally, an executive recruiter will call up an executive on the premise that he is recruiting him. What the recruiter really wants is for the executive he called to hire his search firm to recruit additional employees for the executive's company. This is usually done when an executive recruiter gets wind of an opening at a particular company but does not have any friends or connections employed there. By going through the motions of recruiting the boss of the vacant position, the recruiter will very smoothly let the boss know that he himself is too heavy for any such search assignment.

The recruiter might then casually mention that he has come up with a couple of outstanding candidates for the (mythical) out of town search assignment, but they want to remain local. Before you know it, the recruiter has himself a search assignment, and the boss is probably thinking to himself, "Boy, what a coincidence!"

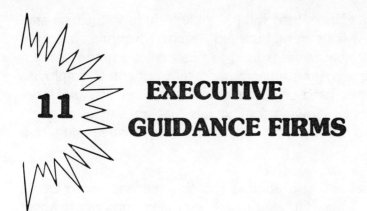

11 EXECUTIVE GUIDANCE FIRMS

These firms tend to have the most creative display ads in the various newspapers. I guess they need all the "sizzle" they can muster when they charge up to $4,000 or more to individuals who come to them for help.

The ads frequently infer that with their experience and "know how" they can land you that top job you always dreamed about. Executive guidance firms tell you that they "will function as your own personal consultant" in dealing with employers. By the time you have listened to their sales pitch, it would not be too difficult to receive the impression that the executive guidance counsellor will "tuck you into bed at night, dress you in the morning, and hold your hand during the interview." Executive guidance firms frequently imply that their techniques never fail—They will help you find a job ". . . no matter how long it takes." They will also tell you that they do not accept just anyone! Ask them who they turned down!

Executive guidance firms will probably include in their several-thousand-dollar fee several hundred resumes. Resumes prepared by executive guidance firms tend to possess a common denominator of "sugar coating" that broadcasts to potential employers that the candidate used an executive guidance firm. Many of these resumes use such glowing testimonials that an employer might easily wonder "If this guy is so fantastic—why is he looking for a job?"

Psychological testing is another tool that guidance firms use in selling their package. Granted, there are many appropriate applications for psychological testing, but what is an engineer, who has been an engineer for twenty-five years, going to benefit from a battery of tests aimed at pinpointing what he is best suited for? In all probability, he is too old to become a fireman.

Executive guidance firms boast of their extensive research sources to assist you in making contacts, and to tell you who to contact within the company. If you use the reference materials which were previously described (in Chapter 5) you should basically be able to accomplish the same goal. About the only difference may be that instead of asking the guidance counsellor, "What's the best way to use a directory?"—you would ask the reference librarian at the public library.

The executive guidance counsellor will often claim that, "The best job opportunities within a company are not being advertised. To get a crack at the best opportunities within a company, you have to get to the top executive who is making the decision about that position before he announces it to everyone else." I agree with a great deal of this philosophy, and that is why I so strongly advocate both a first class mail and telephone campaign aimed at the right executive! The difference is whether you want to handle your campaign yourself—or pay someone else several thousand dollars to assist you.

There may be exceptions, but on the whole executive guidance firms charge several thousand dollars to individuals for simply giving them advice and showing them how to find a job *on their own* . . . but I must not forget to include the pastel-colored resumes and the psychological tests! They do not recruit for companies, nor do they place applicants in jobs. They serve in an advisory capacity to the individual job seeker.

You may be impressed by a particular executive guidance firm—and many of them are easy to be impressed by—on the surface that is. . . . They usually have very plush accommodations, and the counsellors usually convey the impression of being the fatherly senior executive who has been through it all himself and possesses great wisdom (they frequently do—when it comes to coaxing you to sign their contracts). At least with the employment agency you have to receive a job offer before you become obligated under a contract.

With the executive guidance counsellor, you could wind up with no job offers, yet several thousand dollars poorer. At least use the same screening process which was suggested for employment agencies. You probably will not be able to avoid signing their contracts, as you frequently can with employment agencies, but at least demand good references from both the firm and the individual counsellor assigned to you. If they can produce several satisfied clients whom they have recently helped to obtain better jobs—then that guidance firm's efforts may be well worth the fee.

If they are unable to produce any meaningful references—and the only references which would be meaningful would be from individuals who have recently used their services—then politely tell them "no thanks" and head for a good library. . . .

OUTPLACEMENT

Many executive guidance firms market a service to companies which is referred to as *outplacement.* Outplacement is used to help an employee who is being terminated.

At the moment of termination, the outplacement representative is right there to begin assisting the newly fired employee. The executive guidance counsellor puts his services to use right when the employee receives his initial trauma. The idea is to try and make a "painful situation" a little less "painful." The outplacement consultant provides support when the terminated employee really needs it—right in the beginning.

I am in favor of companies using a modified version of outplacement services. They might have someone present the day they fire the individual—because most individuals need to talk to someone who can give them some unemotional, common sense advice.

The terminated executive knows the outplacement consultant is being paid by the company to help him quickly find a job, and possibly reduce some of his severance or salary continuance pay. Many companies, when they fire an executive, will continue to pay the executive for a reasonable time until he finds a new position.

Some executives might not be comfortable at such a time working with a consultant who is being paid by the company. Even if he is not concerned that the guy giving him all this good advice is being paid by the company that has just "fired" him, an executive might prefer to use someone else for help, or just want to conduct his own job search campaign.

The specific modification I suggest is that if companies are willing to spend several thousand dollars for outplacement, then after a couple of days they should give the fired executive the choice of either continuing with the outplace consultant—or receiving the money which the company would have spent with the outplacement firm. He could either spend it with another executive guidance firm of his own choosing, or conduct his own job search campaign and be that much money ahead.

COMBINATION EXECUTIVE GUIDANCE AND PLACEMENT FIRMS

There are some executive guidance firms that charge the applicant a fee (such as ten percent of the lowest salary he would accept), and then proceed to try and place him.

If you are going to consider one of these firms, you absolutely must find out their true "batting average." If you are shooting for $35,000 and pay a firm $3,500 to line you up with an excellent job paying $38,000—then it might not have been such a bad deal. On the other hand, if you pay $3,500 and they then forget about you—you should feel quite "clean" for you have just been "taken to the cleaners."

The names of actually placed clients are a must. Also, obtain the names of the companies where clients were placed, and who they dealt with at those particular companies. If this type of executive guidance firm is on the "up and up", then they should be able to provide good references.

Many of these combination executive guidance-placement firms lead you to believe that they will try to negotiate your fee back from the company when they place you. They will also infer that most of the time they are successful in accomplishing this feat. If they are, and can prove it, then they could be an excellent source to use. If they cannot prove their results, but simply attempt to have you sign on the dotted line of their contract and pay your money—say "goodbye" and leave!

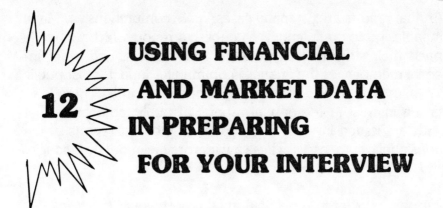

12 USING FINANCIAL AND MARKET DATA IN PREPARING FOR YOUR INTERVIEW

Successful interviews do not happen by chance. Frequently, much preparation on the part of the candidate will take place before the actual interview. Obviously, if the interview is with an executive recruiter who has not yet disclosed his client, then this would not apply.

Find out as much as you can about both the company and the people you will be meeting. If the company is public—that is, its stock is listed on an exchange or listed over the counter—then any number of the previously mentioned sources should be of help.

If you have time, obtain an annual report directly from the company. An annual report alone will arm you with almost everything you need to know about the company—at least for starters prior to the interview.

Annual reports are, in many cases, quite comprehensive. Many companies go to great lengths to publish a report which will really impress their stockholders, potential stockholders, and other influential members of the financial community. In fact, most public companies take a lot of pride in their annual reports. There is so great an interest in the annual reports of public companies that awards are issued in several categories to the best reports of the various public companies. These awards are given out by *Financial World Magazine.*

Items to look for in a public annual report would be:

1. *A description of the company business.* What products do they make, or what services do they provide? What are their trade names? Frequently, the annual report will even indicate how the company stands in the industry. Are they leaders or followers?

2. *Where is the company heading?* Many annual reports will include sales trends, earnings trends, and even share-of-market trends. Is the company really expanding?

3. *Financial data.* How solvent are they? What is their net worth? Do not forget to read the footnotes to the annual report. Frequently, some of the most important information can be in a simple footnote.

4. *Who is running the company?* The annual report will list the company officers and the directors. You can easily see if the company is family controlled—at least in obvious cases, where there are several officers and directors with the same last name.

Is top management young or old? These can all be important factors in your decision-making process. If top management is old, then they might all soon be gone. That could be good or bad. It might provide opportunities for job openings, but it could also mean that someday in the not so distant future the company could be sold—and you could be out of a job! On the other hand, if all the management people are young, that could mean that they are all working very hard to build a great company for the future, and there could be ample career opportunities. But, looking at it another way, if they do not succeed with these great expansion plans, you will not be moving ahead either. It could be frustrating waiting for something good to happen in the way of a promotion—when the boss is younger than you are.

There is an additional report that many public companies file with the Securities and Exchange Commission called the 10-K Report. If you are able to get hold of one, in addition to the annual report, this could provide even more pertinent information on the company. There is, occasionally, information in a 10-K report which is required to be filed, that will not be included in the annual report for various reasons. Sometimes negative information might be handled one way in a 10-K report to the Securities and Exchange Commission, and another in the annual report. The more information you have at your disposal, the better off you are. . . .

Private Companies

Private companies are frequently more difficult to check out. A good source is your own bank. Banks subscribe to various credit services which evaluate companies and industries. If you are a half-way decent customer, your banker should be more than happy to assist you. After all, if you can land a better job—you may become a better customer.

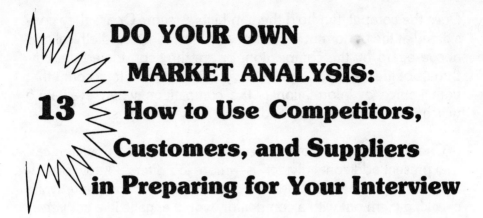

DO YOUR OWN MARKET ANALYSIS:
13 How to Use Competitors, Customers, and Suppliers in Preparing for Your Interview

Another method for checking out any kind of company—whether public or private—is with their competitors, customers, and suppliers. If you have personal contacts with any of these sources, then checking out your new potential employer should be relatively easy. If, however, you are getting ready to be interviewed by a private company and you have no personal contacts with their competitors, customers, or suppliers—you can still check them out!

COMPETITORS

This group can be the most fun! Level with them, and tell them exactly what you are doing. Ask the competitor how your potential employer is looked upon within the industry. Are they leaders, innovators, developers of new products? Or are they also-rans?

103

Does the competition hold them in high esteem? Or are they considered at the bottom of the heap? Are they considered ethical and above-board by the competition, or are they considered the cutthroats of the industry? Obviously, you must take into account that your source of information is the competition when evaluating which information is valid and which is "sour grapes."

Checking out your potential employer with the competition can also present additional dividends—more job offers! I know of several instances where a candidate considering one company, while checking them out with a competitor, would engage in a conversation something like this—Competitor: "They are a fine company. I consider them the second best in our industry. But as long as you are considering our industry, why not consider us, too?" The competitor may proceed to ask you some background questions, and before you know it he will invite you in for an interview.

The mere fact that you are being considered for employment by a competitor makes you all the more valuable. This is especially true when you are considering going to work for the leader of an industry, and checking them out with lower-ranking competitors. If you are good enough to be considered by Number One then you must be pretty good. . . .

In the retail business—restaurants, gas stations, department stores, or whatever—I have heard that the runners-up of a particular group (and these are still major chains) will not even bother to conduct their own store location analysis and marketing research. They simply conclude that if the area is good enough for their industry leader there is no need for money to be spent in researching the area. Number One has already spent the money, and announced their findings by opening up a new store. . . . I guess this attitude explains why so many of them are still looking at the "backside" of the industry leader!

The fact that you are going to the trouble of checking-out your potential employer with the competition has to make a favorable impression on whichever competitor you talk to.

Incidentally, all your initial checking-out should be by telephone.

I have found that people are more candid on the telephone than if they have to submit their comment in writing. Also, as we discussed earlier, you can cover a lot more ground by telephone in a shorter period of time.

CUSTOMERS

Call up the customer purchasing agents, or whoever else does the buying of your potential employer's products, and question them. Ask them about product reliability. How do they rate the quality? Are they dealing with the same people over a period of time? If you are finding it difficult to locate customers, then call the sales manager of the company you are checking-out and ask him to recommend a few.

SUPPLIERS

Call up the sales manager or a salesman of a company supplying your prospective-employer company. Explain your interest, and say you would value any comments they might have. Ask them who else the prospective employer buys from. Are the size and frequency of the orders increasing? If not, why not? Do they pay their bills on time? How is employee turnover? Is it stable? You want to think twice before joining a company which is a revolving door for employees. Keep in mind though, when you are evaluating the information from suppliers, that their "bread is buttered" by the company you are checking out. Former suppliers might be an even better source. . . .

If you arrive for the interview with all the additional knowledge you have gained by doing your own research—you have just got to make a favorable impression on the interviewer! There are not too many things you can do to impress an interviewer as much as modestly and respectfully demonstrating that you have done your homework on the company, and can intelligently discuss the company's business.

An employer may be considering a dozen candidates for a position. If *you* are the one to whom he does not have to keep repeating the same answers to the same routine questions—questions that should have been satisfied prior to the interview—then you have very favorably set yourself apart. You will be able to ask questions which could only be asked by one who was familiar with the company and their industry. Learn the nomenclature, and when appropriate use some of the "buzz words."

Every employer has to be pleased when he feels he is talking to a candidate who knows something about his business. There is nothing positive about saying, "I really do not know anything about your business," and then proceeding to prove it. Who needs to hire someone who is ignorant, when he can hire someone who at least took the time, and made the effort, to learn about the company and their business. Come **prepared** for the interview. . . .

14 DRESSING FOR THE INTERVIEW

The cliche, "You can't tell a book by it's cover," applies to all situations *except job interviews!* Interviewers tend to do the opposite, and judge people *by* their appearance.

Some jobs obviously require a more outstanding physical appearance than others. A vice president of sales has to worry more about his appearance than a research engineer in the laboratory. Even though you may eventually routinely report for work in old clothes while working in a dirty plant, when you apply for that job be prepared to look your best. . . .

Some years ago I was conducting a search for a company in the structural steel fabrication business. I was recruiting an engineering manager for them. An initial interview was set up for a candidate I had recruited from a competitor. We shall refer to him as Brad.

Brad had the same position with the competitor. However, the competing company planned to move their operation to a distant city. Brad was interested in my client's position because he did not want to relocate, and my client was located close to Brad's home.

Everything about Brad's background seemed to be ideally suited for the opening. He had been with his present employer twelve years, starting as a draftsman and ending up as engineering manager. He had completed both a Bachelor of Science degree in Mechanical Engineering and a Master of Business Administration degree at night, over a period of eleven years. I felt that Brad was certain to receive an offer. He was turned down by a recently hired personnel manager who came from another industry!

When I followed up with the Personnel Manager, he indicated that he turned Brad down for some reasons which, to me, did not quite add up. Later, he admitted that the real reason was that Brad showed up for the interview at 7 P.M. looking like a "bum." "He did not bother to clean up before arriving for the interview," claimed the personnel manager, who felt that if Brad had come in the middle of the day he could have excused his appearance, but that there was no excuse for looking as he did at 7 P.M.

What the Personnel Manager failed to learn from Brad was that he arrived for the interview coming directly from work. What had happened was that there had been an accident at the plant that day, and Brad had worked right up until leaving for the interview directing the repairs of some major equipment. In fact, he went back to work that evening after his interview.

Brad should have *explained why* he looked as he did, but did not think it was a "big deal" since anyone in his industry knows that if you work in a structural steel fabrication plant you get dirty. He *assumed* that the Personnel Manager would know he came directly from work, and so did not have an opportunity to change clothes.

I got back to the Personnel Manager and explained the situation to him. He agreed to invite Brad back for a second interview. I made sure that this interview was scheduled first thing in the morning, at 8:30 A.M. I also made sure that Brad arrived directly from home all "spiffy" and wearing a suit. Needless to say, Brad was subsequently hired.

A major error was almost made by my client, simply because the candidate was not dressed properly for his first interview.

Some basic dress and grooming suggestions for men and women follow:

MEN

Hair. In this day and age, you might not want to wear your hair in the close-cropped styles of the fifties, but try not to have it down to your shoulders either. Any man with very long hair who is applying for an executive position is just looking to be turned down.

Top management people tend to be older and more conservative. Do not forget this. People like to surround themselves with others they can relate to. A conservative executive who is doing the hiring, might find it a bit difficult relating to a long haired "hippie." Even if you are not really a "hippie," the fact that you resemble one will cause the same result—*no job offer.*

If you wear a hair piece, make sure it is a good one. If you are losing your hair a *good* hair piece can make you look 100 percent better and several years younger. A cheap one will only make you look like—well, a guy wearing a cheap hair piece. . . .

I suggest making a trip to the barber a day or two before the interview. You will never be criticized for being too well groomed.

If you have a mustache, make sure it is neatly trimmed. Avoid novelty mustaches such as extra long "handlebar" and "Fu-Man-chu" styles. Avoid beards whenever possible. If your appearance is conservative, you will never be criticized. Appear flamboyant, and "red flags" will start popping up in the mind of the interviewer.

109

An exception to the above might apply in an artistic endeavor—as an artist, writer, or musician (if you apply for a job in a rock band wearing a three piece suit, I would imagine the reverse would apply). You have to use good judgement and common sense. Try to project empathy as to how the interviewer envisions the prospective employee.

Colognes, after-shave lotions, and other sweet-smelling creations. Keep the flowery smells to a minimum. A faint, pleasant after-shave scent is fine, but it can really be offensive to the interviewer to smell the candidate as he is walking into his office.

Wear a suit. You just cannot top the appearance of a freshly pressed suit. Conservative sport coats and blazers come in second—but a distant second for certain positions! Vests that match the suit are fine. I mention "match" because if the interview happens to be scheduled on a cold day, I would hate to see you show up for the interview wearing a perfect blue suit coordinated with a bright red wool vest!

Be careful of the extremely loud and bold colors. Try to keep your suit to the basic shades, blues, greys, browns, charcoals, etc. *Conservative* stripes, plaids, checks, solids, are all ideal. Do not show up wearing a business suit which is nice but obviously outdated. If wide lapels are "in," make sure the suit does not have narrow ones, and vice versa.

Avoid leisure suits for interviews. They were a fad that has come and gone. Even when they were "in" they were terrible to wear for business.

I am generally not too enthusiastic about wearing sport coats for interviews. If you must wear one, keep it to the basic conservative blazer, and wear colors such as navy blue or camel. Conservative sport coats in muted shades, stripes, or plaids would probably be just as good as a blazer.

Dress shirts. White dress shirts are always proper. Soft pastel shades are also fine with the properly coordinated suit. Do not

110

worry about stripes if they are not too bold. Avoid too loud a color, whether the shirt is plain or striped. You might also consider checks as a possibility, as long as they are rather sedate. The collar style is optional. If you prefer button-downs, wear them. If you prefer spread-collars or pin-collars—OK.

Ties. Use common sense in selecting your tie. Avoid a clashing bright color. Select one that blends in with your shirt and suit. *Slightly* bright is as daring as I'll recommend. Save your wild ties for socializing—not interviewing. *Bow ties are out*—unless you plan on showing up for the interview wearing a tuxedo, and I don't recommend that! String ties are not recommended either (unless, perhaps, you are applying for a job as a tour guide at some "wild west" amusement attraction).

Socks. Should be dark colors that blend in with the pants and shoes. Solids are usually a lot safer than patterns. If you have trouble separating colors in the morning, have someone check to make sure you are not wearing brown socks with your blue suit!

Shoes. Should also be appropriate for the suit worn to the interview. Solid black, brown, or cordovan colors, are fine. It makes no difference whether the shoe is a wing tip, moccasin toe, plain, or cap toe. Dress loafers are OK if they are neat and dressy-looking. No penny loafers! Avoid exaggerated heels—you are not going dancing. Also, keep all sport shoes and most boots in the closet. Some boots might be acceptable—if they are really dress boots. Do not forget to *shine your shoes.* "Scuffy" shoes look terrible!

Handkerchiefs. In the jacket pocket they are fine, providing they are either white or color-coordinated with the shirt and or tie. Keep another handkerchief or tissue, in another pocket, for actual use.

Outer-coat. Can either be an allweather type, or a good conservative woolen one. Avoid short lengths and jackets. Tan allweather coats always look smart, as do camel, blue, black, and charcoal woolen topcoats and overcoats. Herringbone wools in

111

grey and charcoal are also ideal, as are cashmeres and dressy leathers.

Hats. As far as I am concerned, they are optional. Some guys look great in them, while others look terrible. If you do not feel comfortable with one on—then skip it. If you do wear one, color-coordinate it with your outer-coat. Also, make sure you are not wearing an old one from your college days with a dated brim size. Avoid caps. Western style hats may be OK on certain occasions in the Western part of the country, but for the rest of the U.S., wear a dress hat—if any.

Belts. A belt should be conservative and color-coordinated with your suit. Avoid big buckles and keep it simple. Some men feel more comfortable wearing suspenders—if you do, stick to solid colors.

Jewelry. A nice watch is fine, but avoid novelty watches—you do not want anything to distract the interviewer. No chains should be worn around the neck. Keep rings to a minimum and avoid big flashy diamonds (if you happen to own one). One ring per hand—so if you wear a wedding band that is all you should be wearing on your left hand. On the right hand you might want to wear a not-too-flashy dress ring. Try to avoid rings which denote any particular religious affiliation.

Glasses. If you need to wear glasses, then *wear them.* People look silly when they attempt to do simple things without their glasses on, when they should be wearing them.

If you wear sun glasses, do not enter the waiting room still wearing them—lets not go "Hollywood." Also, I have a strong prejudice against obviously tinted prescription glasses. I think they are hideous and make your eyes look "funny"!

Briefcase. When you walk into the office carrying an attaché or briefcase, it should add to your appearance—not detract. Invest in an expensive looking case. A beat-up, old, or cheap one is as bad as shoes that need shining!

WOMEN

Hair.   Hair must be well groomed. It does not matter whether you wear long hair or short. It should be neat and clean looking. If you color your hair, make sure you have a first class job. Blonde hair with dark roots showing looks awful—and lazy! If you wear a wig, make sure it looks like real hair. Invest in a good one—because cheap wigs usually look that way!

Cosmetics.   Use make-up very carefully. Sloppily made-up or overly-made up women look awful, but one who knows how to select and apply her make-up well looks great every day. If you are not too adept with make-up, then have someone help you. You do not want to make a poor impression, just because your make-up looks bad.

Colognes and perfumes.   Go easy! A light, pleasant scent is fine, but you want to avoid wearing strong scents. Also, cheap perfumes have a tendency to smell that way. Wear a good quality cologne or perfume.

Jewelry.   Jewelry should complement your outfit. Avoid gaudy jewelry. Also, avoid too expensive jewelry. There may be an appropriate time to flaunt the big diamond—but the interview is not it. You would not want to appear richer than the boss—would you?

Dresses and suits.   Neat, conservative dresses and suits are best for interviews. I do not like pant suits for job interviews. Avoid wild patterns and colors. Also, avoid the plunging neckline—it may offend the interviewer if the interviewer is a female, and distract the male interviewer. For the same basic reasons, make sure your clothes fit well—not too tight or too loose.

Stockings.   Should obviously be in good taste and coordinate with the rest of your outfit. No fancy mesh weaves or bright colors. Neutral flesh tones are best. Summer or winter—*wear stockings.*

Shoes.   Should be dressy heels. How high or how low depends on how tall you are. No extreme, high-fashion shoes. Best materials are leather or suede. Dressy boots are also acceptable. Neutral colors, for shoes or boots, are best.

Handbags.   Should either match the shoes, or coordinate with them. No extreme styles or gaudy colors.

Outerwear.   Dress coats are excellent, as are allweather coats. Tasteful wools and wool-blends look best. If you own a fur . . . there is such a thing as over dressing . . . leave it at home. (I suggest that any man who wears a fur ought to leave it at home too!)

Hats and gloves.   Should either match, or coordinate with, the coat and shoes. Make sure you are on the conservative side in selecting your hat—if you choose to wear one. You do not want to look as if you are getting ready for the vaudeville stage.

Briefcase.   There are many good-looking briefcases designed for women. Invest in a good one, if you do not already own one.

Glasses.   Basically the same comments as made earlier for the men. Avoid wearing sun glasses into the office. Avoid extreme tinted shades. I have seen some really wild shapes and styles of womens' glasses; but be conservative—be stylish, but not outlandish. But, if you need to wear glasses—*wear them.* Do not leave them at home because you feel they do not look good. You will look a lot worse bumping into a door!

Proper dress for an interview boils down to *good taste and common sense.* Your clothes and accessories are your outer packaging. We all know how valuable good packaging is to the sale of products. We all probably have purchased products, at one time or another, based on packaging. You—about to have that interview—are a very important product. *Be packaged well!*

15 PSYCHOLOGICAL TESTING AND THE INDUSTRIAL PSYCHOLOGIST

Psychological testing, sometimes affectionately referred to as "having your head shrunk," is a process which is used by a substantial number of employers. The psychological test could be given as easily prior to the interview, at the midpoint of the interview, or at the end. Everyone who administers psychological tests has their own theory as to when to give them.

I had one client company where the vice president of personnel was a psychologist. He designed his own psychological test battery, which took approximately two hours to administer. Every candidate considered for *any* position, whether there for a potential vice president's job or the lowest hourly worker, had to complete the test. What was bad was that the test had to be taken before anyone was interviewed. This would frequently alienate potentially good employees. Many people are not keen on taking these tests, and would prefer to know more about the position before they "submit to the grind." It would make more sense to administer the same test *after* the candidate has had an opportunity to be sold somewhat on the company. It is a little like "putting the cart before the horse." In many instances a lot of valuable time could be saved by testing after the interview.

I have had company clients tell me that they really believe in psychological testing. These companies believe that their own tests are valid, and that high scores on them equates to high probable success on the job.

Other company clients have used psychological tests, but dropped them after a period of time. They did not feel that they were worth the effort. These companies felt that there was very little validity in the results of the tests and corresponding results on the job.

Psychological testing, if used properly, can be a definite positive tool in the hiring process. As an example, I have seen psychological tests identify serious psychological and medical problems about a candidate which went undetected by both the recruiter and the company. This could happen in extreme cases where the candidate could initially camouflage a serious problem, but the combination of psychological testing and follow-up interview with an industrial psychologist would uncover it.

What is so important is the kind of written tests used, how they are interpreted, and that there are personal follow-up sessions with the industrial psychologist included. To have just a battery of written questions, with the answers simply added up by a clerk, the score graphed and forwarded to the executive making the hiring decision—this is only doing a partial job.

Believe it or not, there are definite benefits to be gained by the individual candidate who is subjected to a first class psychological testing session.

The one outstanding example which stands out in my mind concerned a candidate I recruited for a home building subsidiary of a Fortune 500 company. I will refer to him as Carl. The position was Vice President of Sales. The client was involved in about six projects, all within 150 miles of each other. Carl was at that time working for another home builder who also had all developments within easy driving distance of each other.

When I recruited Carl, he indicated that he was about to be promoted to Regional Sales Vice President over a much broader geographic area (about twelve states), but he was still definitely interested in my assignment. Prior to his present position, he was working for another real estate developer—also ready to promote him to a multi-state responsibility when he left. I might mention that Carl's accomplishments in both positions were significant, and his references were impeccable.

The industrial psychologist was able to determine that Carl had a severe fear of flying. Here was a top sales executive in the home building industry who had never been up in an airplane. The few times with his present and prior employers when he had to attend to business affairs at significant distances away—he simply made excuses for driving or taking the train. The only reason that Carl was considering my position was to avoid ever getting on an airplane. He had left his prior position for the same reason.

Carl did not readily admit to this fear, or for that fear being the reason behind prior job change and present interest. In fact, I do not think he ever disclosed the complete story to anyone . . . including his wife! This particular industrial psychologist was able to get my candidate to admit that his fear of flying at least played a *partial* role in his prior job changes. The psychologist told Carl that he was going to recommend that my client *not* hire him—because the new position could, in the near future, open up new projects, and Carl would just leave again. . . . Carl opened up! He told the industrial psychologist that he was the first person to detect his fear and the role it played in his prior job change and present job interest . . . that his phobia was really the *only reason* for the change!

I am happy to report that the industrial psychologist referred Carl to another psychologist who specialized in helping people overcome their fear of flying. Today, Carl is National Sales Vice President for the same company he was with when I recruited him.

Oh yes, he completed his fear of flying sessions with the psychologist, and last year flew over 100,000 miles. I understand that now, even on vacations where he does not have to fly, Carl actually prefers flying to the other modes of transportation.

Company insight can also be gained through an industrial psychologist. The working environment at various companies is as unique as the people who work for them. For some companies, to work overtime is truly a rarity. For others, overtime is the norm. Some companies manage by objective . . . others by aggression! Maybe your personality will or will not mesh with the prospective employer. Without forgetting that the industrial psychologist is being paid by the company—and so not getting too carried away— discuss some characteristics of the prospective employer's style of management. Do people stay long? If not, why not? Does top management delegate authority with responsibility? Probing questions and answers are even more important where one or two individuals truly dominate a company.

If the meeting with the industrial psychologist is done right, you might find out some valuable information about the company— even while the psychologist is appraising you.

Taking psychological tests can be tricky. Assume they are administered, written, and evaluated by experts, and the best approach is good judgement and common sense. Many questions are asked in several different ways and at different times. You probably won't realize that this is happening.

My general advice for taking psychological tests is to get a good night's sleep the night before, and just be yourself. Trying to be too clever will most likely just get you into trouble. A good industrial psychologist can spot a phony right away. Be candid, sincere, and respectful. If you do not believe in psychological testing, it is all right to be candid and sincere—but do not be stupid and relay all these great thoughts to the psychologist—he, too, probably has a wife, kids, and a mortgage. . . .

118

Do not be afraid to discuss your written test results with the psychologist. If the test was important enough to take—then it might be interesting to know the results. Most psychologists should be happy to discuss your results upon request. They may not tell you everything. After all, some of their analysis might be considered privileged information, but if they are going to recommend you for hire, they should want to maintain goodwill by at least giving you a basic idea of your strengths and weaknesses.

Psychological testing is a "tool" and most companies regard it as such. Some companies go overboard and place too much weight on the results, while others totally ignore them. I have known cases where candidates were strongly *not recommended* for hire, and were hired anyway—even though not the son-in-law of the company President!

Industrial psychologists become valuable when the employer is "sitting on the fence" concerning the hiring of a candidate. His input could easily push the decision either way.

Written tests are sometimes administered right away, but the personal interview with the industrial psychologist usually comes towards the end of the hiring process. If the company is not at least mildly interested, then they will not spend the several hundred dollars it costs for testing. When the candidate is sent to the industrial psychologist, he has usually approached the "home stretch." Many companies will only send one candidate at a time to the industrial psychologist. If he passes, then they proceed to the physical exam, more references if required, and, hopefully, on to the offer!

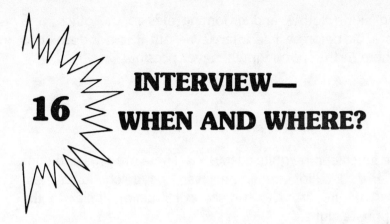

16 INTERVIEW— WHEN AND WHERE?

WHEN

This is a very significant consideration for many people. For most individuals, I would recommend scheduling interviews first thing in the morning. Most people feel and look fresher in the morning— and since offers and turn downs are sometimes decided by the smallest of factors, make use of even the slightest advantage.

No man would want to show up for a 5:00 P.M. interview wearing a "5 o'clock shadow."

Women who get up at the crack of dawn to do their hair, and whatever else they do to look attractive at the office, are just defeating their purpose when they schedule an interview right after a long, tough day at the office. . . . Of course, both men and women could bring extra clothes and grooming aids to the office, and freshen up a bit before a late interview—but it is a lot easier to schedule them in the morning, whenever possible.

WHERE

That free lunch can be quite costly. . . . There are pros and cons to the preferred locations for interviews. I have scheduled them everywhere, ranging from an on-site construction trailer to the swankiest private clubs.

There is nothing wrong with being interviewed over lunch or dinner providing:

1. The restaurant selected is appropriate for a comfortable private conversation. It is just not satisfactory to have an interview over lunch where it is noisy, crowded, and the tables are so close that your elbows are practically touching the diners next to you. This kind of setting utterly ruins any hope of a good interview! You must have both comfort and privacy for an effective interview.

2. If you are going to be interviewed over dinner, then make sure your table manners are good. Trying to impress the interviewer with a mouth full of food just will not work. Some people can handle dinner conversation very smoothly, while others come off looking very sloppy and awkward.

3. Can you maintain your edge with as little as one drink? Some of us can while some of us cannot. If one drink has *any* negative effect on you whatsoever, then do not drink at all just before or during the interview! On the other hand, one drink might make you relax and feel better during the interview. You have to be your own judge.

Do not fear offending the interviewer by declining any alcohol. If he asks "Do you drink?" you might say, "Just on special occasions." Some positions call for a significant amount of customer entertaining, where alcohol is usually served. If you are being interviewed for such a position, and have successfully handled customers and clients with a couple of drinks at dinner in the past, then enjoy yourself. Indicating you do not drink to the interviewer when you really do, can possibly hurt you more in that situation than having a drink or two. On the other hand, if you never drink—even with customers and clients—for gosh sakes, do not start now!

If the interviewer declines a drink at dinner, then you do the same—even if you would really like one. . . . Many people who do not drink are offended when someone else does. Let good judgement and common sense prevail.

   4.   If the interviewer does not smoke, let that be a message. If you are a smoker but see no telltale signs that the interviewer is one too, then always ask, "Do you mind if I smoke?" It makes no difference whether you smoke cigarettes, cigars, or pipe. In fact, if you suspect that the interviewer does not smoke, I would suggest that you do not bring up the subject and do not smoke during the interview. There are some people who are so offended by smokers, that they might not hire you for that reason alone.

If the interview is over lunch or dinner, be considerate and do not smoke at the table before the food is served. An exception might be made if the interviewer smokes before dinner—then you may go ahead. Same thing applies after dinner. Anyone who smokes *during* dinner ought to "be hung out to dry."

If you feel that you will have a "nicotine fit" if you do not smoke during the interview, then go ahead and ask. Most likely the interviewer will say "go ahead," but again use *good judgement and common sense.*

If you *must* smoke during an interview, then limit your smoking to cigarettes. Cigars smell too strongly—unless the interviewer is smoking one too.

I know a secretary who has her boss's ear when he is about to make a hiring decision. The boss is national sales manager for a food company. The secretary has confided to me that she would never let a cigar smoker be hired. She told me that over the years she has eliminated some outstanding candidates—just because they arrived for the interview smoking a cigar. She always finds some logical reason to recommend another candidate. She cannot stand the smell of cigars. . . .

Pipes are too disruptive—unless the interviewer is also smoking one. I have heard of instances where individual managers will not hire a pipe smoker. They seem to feel that pipe smokers are too theoretical and are not "doers." As ludicrous as this bias may be, when you know that some correctable habit may offend an interviewer, correct it and so increase your odds for a job offer.

MISCELLANEOUS ADVICE

If you happen to have an interview take place at the employer's office, here are a couple of suggestions:

Men should be friendly—but strictly business—with the boss's secretary. No wise guy flirtations! She may be superficially receptive, but chances are all you did was encourage her to report back to her boss that you tried to "come on" to her. She may make it sound much worse than it actually was. So, never mix business and pleasure. . . .

If you have to wait in the outer office for a few minutes, do not just sit there like "a bump on a log." Bring something with you to read, or at least grab a magazine which will probably be available. Having made you wait fifteen or twenty minutes—and then coming out to find you slouched in your seat doing absolutely nothing—will not impress the boss with your ability to manage your time well.

No matter where your interview is held, always show up just a few minutes before the interview is scheduled. Arriving five to ten minutes early is perfect. Arriving right on time is OK, but playing it too close. Arriving late is absolutely terrible! Obviously, being a few minutes late is not as terrible as an hour, but do not assume that arriving a few minutes late is all right, because it is *not*. Arriving late causes a negative impression "right off the bat." Why start an interview being in the hole?

124

If you see that you are going to be even a few minutes late, then by all means have the common sense to call ahead and let the interviewer know that you will be late. This is obviously not as good as arriving on time, but at least it shows you have used some common courtesy.

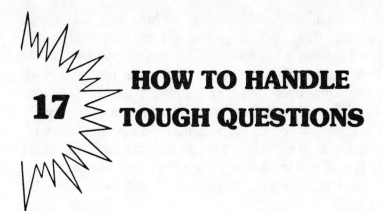

17 HOW TO HANDLE TOUGH QUESTIONS

Rarely does a candidate get interviewed by an employer without having some "curves" thrown at him. Everyone is vulnerable to "loaded" or "curve" questions. This is especially true if there is some red flag on your resume to call attention to a particularly delicate subject. Some "tough" questions may be triggered by the following pointers:

Several jobs in a short period of time. The best defense is an offense. Head the interviewer off at the pass! As long as the "Dates Employed" are glaring at him from the resume, you should explain why you had so many jobs before he even asks. Make sure you explain the reasons in a manner which makes sense. Be positive—even when discussing a negative subject.

For instance, suppose you were fired for incompetence after just one year on a particular job. Depending on how long ago it was, you might indicate that, "Although the job did not work out, I gained quite a bit from it because . . ." and then proceed to tell why. You might also list some accomplishments you achieved, even though you were there only a short time. You may have also taken some additional courses to help improve your background—so that you will be better prepared the next time around. Make sure you are coming across in a sincere manner. You must use empathy. For all you know the same thing may have happened to the interviewer at one time. Avoid the "bull"—candor is refreshing!

Weak formal education.   Turn the liability into an asset. Explain the responsibilities you had when you were young, and how you have studied on your own. You must have, or else you would not have got where you are today—where ever that is. . . . You might indicate, if it is true, that no matter where you were employed you were usually the only non-college graduate at your job level. If there is a possibility of night school, then tell that to the interviewer.

What are your long-range goals?   This question seems to baffle a lot of people. What ever you do, avoid indicating that "What I really want, is a business of my own" . . . even if you do! Employers like to feel that they hire employees "till death do us part." You certainly will not "turn on" any employer by telling him that you will give him the privilege of training you for a couple of years—but you then plan on going out on your own and competing with him. You may even change your own mind once you begin to work for the company.

Companies hate to admit that they hire a lot of people for "dead end" jobs; and then cannot understand why the employees leave as they do. Companies would be a lot better off if they did more of what might be called "cross pollination." After a period of time an employee who has been on the same job switches with someone who has been on a different job about the same length of time. What is accomplished is that two employees are given new motivations and new challenges! Every job has a tendency to become dull

128

after a while—or at least not as exciting as it was in the beginning. If there is not a legitimate promotion available, then create a new stimulus.

Many companies are now beginning to set up programs where they recognize these problems. It is a lot cheaper to switch two employees around, than to replace them both in the market place—when they both become frustrated and quit!

Answer the "long-range goal" question as you really believe . . . outside of "leaving the company." If you feel that some day you could become President of the company, then tell the interviewer so. Also, give him some reason to support your ambitious plans. Maybe you plan on obtaining your MBA, or some other positive accomplishment to help you meet your goals.

What is your greatest weakness? Nobody is perfect. When answering this question, you had better use empathy.

I will never forget the candidate I recruited once for the position of Corporate Controller who told the President of the company that, "My greatest weakness is detail. I hate detail work!" Needless to say, that particular candidate was not hired. The irony of it all was that he had been a successful controller for almost fifteen years. Be honest, but try to think of a "greatest single weakness" which will not immediately eliminate you from any further consideration for the job. . . .

Physical handicaps or health problems. Not everyone is blessed with perfect health or appearance. If you have an obvious physical handicap or health problem, it is usually best to discuss it openly with the interviewer, providing it will not automatically disqualify you for the job. Use empathy and be honest, both with the employer and yourself.

I recommended a candidate to a client once, who was born with only one arm. I will call him Art. He was being considered for the position of Treasurer in a medium sized manufacturing company. His attitude was marvelous. Before I met Art, the individual who recommended him to me had never mentioned his handicap, so I decided to let him mention it rather than having to ask about it myself.

Art mentioned it in due time, and explained how it had never hindered him in any way. In fact, Art explained, because of his handicap he felt he always tried to strive a little harder to overcome it and most successfully did so.

Art was hired by my client and is still successfully employed there as the company's Chief Financial Officer.

Divorce. This is a common subject which, when discussed with applicants, causes discomfort—especially if there are children involved. Unfortunately, in our society today, divorce has become all too common! Some companies will not touch a divorced candidate until after the so-called "adjustment period" is completed—whatever that is. . . . Some people never completely adjust, while others were never completely adjusted to marriage—and become much better right after the divorce.

Approximately fourteen years ago, when I began in the personnel business, there was a definite stigma attached to a divorced person. Today, I believe there is none. How can you have a stigma, when almost forty percent of new marriages are ending in divorce?

The trepidation that employers sometimes have for the recently divorced is that any new job requires total concentration and commitment. If a new employee has to tackle, simultaneously, the adjustment to a new job plus putting life back together after a recent divorce, then the pressures may be too great.

When the subject comes up in an interview, it is best to be candid about it. If the divorce is fairly recent, try to be positive and explain to the interviewer that your marital problems are over, and you are now prepared to give one hundred and ten percent to his job opening. Be positive!

Recently retired military officers. Some employers go out of their way to hire them, while others treat them the same as

130

everyone else. The typical "curve" question that might be asked of a recently retired military officer: "Do you think you may have difficulty adapting to civilian life?" You might respond by explaining that "The responsibility and exposure that I had in the military are directly applicable for the following reasons . . ." then proceed to explain those reasons. Try to draw analogies between what you accomplished in the military—and what you feel the job requires. You might indicate that the same experience in civilian life could be earning you a lot more money—and therefore require a lot more.

When the employer brings up the fact that you are earning a handsome retirement salary, and therefore should not require too much money from him—you have two choices:

1.   Agree and take what he offers, even though it is lower than the going rate for the position involved. Some employers cannot resist trying to take advantage of a retired military man's pension.

2.   Indicate, politely but firmly, that "My pension pay should have no bearing as to the salary the employer has set for the vacant position. I will contribute as much to the company as someone who is not on a pension, and therefore I should be compensated appropriately." This should set the employer straight.

Try to avoid military expressions and "lingo" during the interview. It could be annoying to the interviewer to constantly hear expressions like "10-4", "check" instead of "yes", "negative" instead of "no", the 24-hour clock instead of A.M.s and P.M.s, and the word "Sir" after every "yes" or "no."

The interviewer may not have had an illustrious military career, and hearing all that military jargon might bring back some unpleasant memories. You want to convince the interviewer that your military experience is an asset in fulfilling the requirements of the job. Use civilian terminology which you know will be positive to the interviewer. You want the employer to think of you as a "business executive" rather than a "retired military officer looking for a way to spend his free time."

Minorities.   Many employers will ignore the fact that you are of a minority group, but others will try to test your attitudes and philosophies. If you are ever asked the question: "Do you find it a handicap being [Black/Latino/...] in a management position, supervising non-minorities?" You might answer a question like that by saying, "So far, I have found my being a minority group member is neither a handicap nor an asset in supervising non-minorities. I find that people respect you for what you are, and not for the color of your skin." You might further elaborate: "I have advanced my career over the years by preparing myself for my job, doing the job well, and treating all people fairly."

As time goes on, I find that racial, religious, sexual, age, and other discriminatory barriers really are disappearing—and rightfully so.

Women executives. In many industries and companies it makes no difference whether the executive hired is male or female. However, if you are female and being considered for an executive position, you must still convince the employer that you are *even better* than your male competitors for the job. If you are asked the typical question—"Do you find being a female executive in our industry much of a handicap?", you might respond: "Being a *female* executive might even be an *asset*. The people I deal with have to reason that I have achieved what I have by my abilities and what I can contribute. Once people get to know you, it makes little difference whether you are male or female, but rather—can you get the job done?"

Age. This is a subject that at one stage all of us are glad to discuss with an employer—but as we grow older we know it can possibly hinder us.

I have known executives who act old while still in their thirties. I have known others, in their seventies, who act and think young. I believe in the adage "you are only as old as you feel."

If you are "middle aged"—and I am not sure I know what being "middle aged" is—how do you handle the interviewer who asks "Do you feel you are slowing down because of your age?" or "How many more years do you plan on working before retirement?" Your response might be: "I have never felt better. My resume will illustrate that my most recent years have demonstrated the most growth." Be prepared to substantiate this statement. Highlight your achievements over your most recent years. As for retirement, you indicate that you have no plans for it.

Fortunately, with the new Federal Retirement Law being raised to 70 years of age, this will raise by a few years the length of time employees can work . . . before being declared "obsolete." If you sense some apprehension about your age from the interviewer, you might want to point out the following:

1. The average age of the justices who serve on the United States Supreme Court is older than the retirement age of many companies. If men this old are allowed to serve in one of the most responsible positions in the Country, then maybe it takes time to develop a little wisdom. . . .

2. Colonel Sanders was well into his sixties before he started Kentucky Fried Chicken. He is still going strong today—well into his eighties.

3. Ray Kroc founded McDonald's Corporation when he was in his fifties. He, too, is still active well into his seventies.

4. There is a successful company in South Norwalk, Connecticut, called *Fertl, Inc.* They are in the horticultural products business. Hoyt Catlin is the President, and almost all of his employees are beyond normal retirement age. He feels that older employees are more dependable. Hoyt Catlin is 87 years young. . . .

I remember conducting a search once for a plant manager for a structural steel firm. A candidate was referred to me by someone in the industry only as being "a darn good man." The source did not give me any other background, except where he worked. We will refer to him as Ted. I telephoned Ted long distance, and proceeded to introduce myself and go through my standard recruiting pitch. Before I got very far Ted stopped me to ask if I knew how old he was. I told him I had no idea—which was the absolute truth. He proceeded to tell me, with much pride in his voice, that he was 76 years old.

Ted had retired eleven years ago, when he had completed thirty six years of service, only because of company policy. Six months after retirement Ted was preparing to start another little business, when his employer asked if he would come back and run the plant. They had gone through two plant managers in those six months, and felt they must either split the function in two—or hire Ted back!

Ted received a terrific raise in returning to his old job, and now has no plans to retire. He also said that if he ever did leave his employer after, now, 47 years—it would only be to start his own business! Ted said, "retirement is a waste of time. . . ."

Companies are realizing that what they really need are employees who can successfully do the job—and so why waste a lot of time and money looking for the All American Candidate with fifteen years experience, who is still under thirty, and whose ancestors arrived on the *Mayflower.* The demand for talented management and professional people is so great that companies are rapidly finding that to be discriminatory in their hiring practices is not only immoral and against the law, but makes no economic sense either!

Unemployed Executive.   If you are unemployed and there is no way you can cover yourself with your prior employer—like remaining on the payroll, then just "come clean" and indicate that you are unemployed . . . but have several offers pending.

It just does not pay to try and cover yourself with the old "I am presently doing consulting" routine, unless you really are. Any astute employer will see right through your facade, and you will only weaken your position that much more. He may even ask who some of your clients are, and want to check with them.

One approach you may consider is that you found it very difficult taking time off from work to explore other opportunities. You felt that as long as your prior employer was paying you—you owed him a fair day's work. Rather than have to lie and connive for time off—you "nipped it in the bud," and for better or for worse you elected to pursue your job campaign on a full time basis.

134

18 CRITICAL QUESTIONS WHICH SHOULD BE ANSWERED DURING THE INTERVIEW

Why Is The Position Available?

The executive recruiter may have already told you, but get it from the "horse's mouth." If the employer confirms what the intermediary told you—then fine. If not, then you had better find out why the discrepancy exists.

There are positive as well as negative reasons for a position vacancy. The best positive reason is expansion. This is the best reason in the world to hire additional personnel. A retirement or promotion, with no available individual to promote into the position, would be fine too. Find out, though, if the retirement was planned or sudden. In other words, was the former job holder forced out?

Another negative reason is a position created because of re-trenchment. Yes, companies sometimes will eliminate two or three jobs, and create one new one to accomplish the same work. Watch out for that trap! The pieces must fit, or avoid the opportunity—or so-called opportunity.

If someone left the position, or was terminated, try to find out why. You might even discreetly find out his name, and talk to the individual directly. An employee who has recently left the company is in a position to impart valuable information to someone who is considering joining the same. As Holiday Inn says, "The best surprise is no surprise."

Be leery when the opening is to replace an individual who does not yet know he is about to "get the axe." The reasons may be perfectly valid, but check them out to see if they are valid. Do not forget to use discretion when checking out the reason someone is about to be terminated. You certainly do not want to be the one who causes him to find out the bad news. He will know in due time. Sometimes companies even change their mind about firing an employee—when they see what they would have to replace him with, and how much it would cost.

How Many Employees Have Held This Position in How Long a Period of Time?

You want to avoid getting into a "revolving door" situation. If five people have held this position in three years, then the probability of your ever receiving a "gold watch" is small.

Sometimes many people have held a position over a short period—but now new top management is "calling the shots." If this is the case, you at least have an even chance of eventually earning the "gold watch."

How Does the Boss See This Position?

Is it a "dead end" job, or is there high visibility with lots of opportunities for advancement? Where have other employees gone from this position—Out or up? Does the boss have a high opinion of the importance of this position? Job titles can be deceiving.

What Are the Job Responsibilities and How Much Authority Does It Carry?

Ask to see a job description. See if it matches how the boss describes it. What functions report to the position? If you are going to be called a Manager, whom are you going to manage?

If you have to go through layers of red tape for the most minor decision, obviously this job does not carry much weight. On the other hand, if the position carries with it substantial responsibility and authority—then it should be considered a pretty important position by company top management.

What Is the Title of the Position?

Usually a level of importance which correlates to the position is denoted in the job title. Do not be fooled though, some companies are not that big on "titles." At others, if your card does not say "Vice President," this probably means you are an "assistant file clerk."

How Does the Boss See Himself Within the Company?

Will you be attaching yourself to a "shining star," or are you getting yourself associated with the "black sheep" of the company? This might be more important than you realize. You do not want to be guilty by association. If your potential boss appears genuinely happy and enthusiastic about both his work and the company, and has a generally high self esteem—then this is positive. If he is crying on your shoulder, while at the same time trying to coax you into joining his mess—forget it! The company may be great, but if you are not hired by "the guys wearing white hats," you may find yourself out on the street when top management finally cleans house.

Compensation and Fringe Benefits

Since you probably want to know—there is a way to *properly* ask about compensation and fringe benefits. Once the interview has progressed to the point where you feel the interviewer has had an opportunity to ask you pertinent information, and you have done the same, you might ask, "What is the salary range for the position?"

There is nothing wrong in confirming the salary range on the first interview, but only when you have already completed the other basic trading of information. It would be nice to have the employer interested in hiring you—before you discuss salary. It is most important, however, to know both the range of the starting salary, and the salary range of the job itself.

Why waste your time with a second interview if the job does not pay a favorable salary? Also, you certainly do not want to accept a position where you will be starting at the maximum salary for the job.

Fringe benefits are also important. They must be carefully weighed in determining just what starting salary you would settle for.

You obviously do not want to force the employer's hand as to what he would specifically offer you—but just for a general salary range of the job, and a general policy regarding fringe benefits. If you do not ask—then you will not know to the very end, when you are talking salary in specific terms rather than generalities.

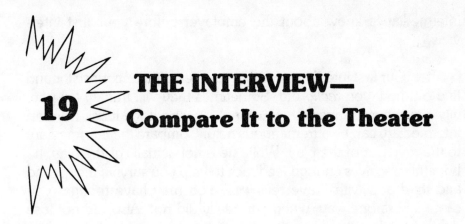

19 THE INTERVIEW—
Compare It to the Theater

Dress Rehearsal

You might compare the interview process to a three act Play—complete with dress rehearsal. The dress rehearsal takes place when you use either an executive search firm, employment agency, or an executive guidance firm. By using an intermediary, you can have your dress rehearsal before your actual performance with the employer. If there is some improvement or correction you can make, then one of the intermediaries is able to give you a valuable piece of constructive criticism.

As an example, you may have a slightly annoying habit of not looking at whoever you are talking to. Poor eye contact is just a poor habit. If you are using an intermediary, then take full advantage of his position and skills. Ask him if there is anything you can do to enhance your chances for being selected. Find out what the intermediaries know about the employer before your first interview.

After your first interview, contact your recruiter or counsellor and find out how you *really* did. Sometimes they will frankly tell you, while in other instances they will not. A candid feedback from an intermediary can be a tremendous help. Compare the intermediary to the reviewer of the play. While he is not actually *at* the play, he hopefully receives enough feedback to help you survive the second and third acts with "rave reviews." You may have thought you came across one way, when you really did not. Also, do not lose sight of the fact that both the executive recruiter and the employment counsellor are typically paid by the company. They may not be in a position to be completely candid with you. Sometimes yes, sometimes no. At least you can receive *some* feedback and make your own judgement.

Act I

The stage is set when you arrive for the interview—no matter where it is held. Let us assume that the initial interview with the employer is held at the company offices. You might consider what you are wearing as your costume for your role—wear it well. . . .

The secretary will likely greet you, and ask you to be seated. If you are wearing an outercoat, she will probably ask if she can hang it up for you. She may even offer you a cup of coffee. If you accept, make sure you do not spill it all over yourself! This may sound ridiculous, but I can think of two instances over the years where my candidates spilled coffee all over themselves while waiting to begin the interview. In another case, it was the secretary who did the spilling—come to think of it, that candidate was a cigar smoker whom I recruited for the position where the secretary would not allow cigar smokers to be hired! None of these candidates were hired.

A few minutes will pass, then the boss will either make his main entrance, or the secretary will escort you into the inner office and the action begins.

140

Both of you will extend warm greetings, while at the same time registering initial reactions to each other. You may be thinking, "Gee, he sure sounded older on the telephone," while the employer may be registering, "He sure looks a lot older in person. I'd better check his age again." At the same time you will be taking in, and evaluating, his office—on a scale of one to ten it may rate eight, which is pretty good. In other words, in those first few seconds of initial contact human nature takes over. You will begin to size each other up. You will note whether his desk is orderly, while the employer may be noticing the "spit shine" on your shoes. This process is all part of the initial impression when meeting face to face. *It is very important.* If the first impression is favorable, then the subsequent steps of the interviewing process seem so much easier. On the other hand, if your appearance is negative you have an uphill battle on your hands!

The employer, no doubt, will ask you to pull up a chair. These are the "props" on the "stage." Do not grab the wrong one! Depending on the size of his office, and how many chairs he has, chair selection should not be a problem. If there are several chairs, then see where he leads you and pick a comfortable one that will place both of you in a good eye-contact position. Do not pick a chair across a table with a big pot of flowers or an ornament which could distract from the interview. Do not select a chair too far away, where both of you would have difficulty seeing and hearing the other.

Make sure the employer sits in the better of the two chairs, if they are not of equal quality. You do not want to give the impression that you are trying to dominate, no matter how slightly.

The employer may begin by making small talk. He may offer you a cup of coffee—if you have not already received one. If you drink coffee, accept it. The cup could also serve as a useful prop. Talking about the weather, or whatever, in the beginning is good. You will both be more relaxed before you get down to the subject matter at hand.

He may break the ice by suggesting that he begin the interview by telling you a little bit about the company. This is great. If you have done your homework, you will be presented with opportunities to carefully communicate responses to his company scenario. You do not interrupt him, but occasionally make an intelligent comment on what he is saying. Gingerly use a few "buzz" words, but do not get carried away. All you want to do, is to let him know that you are interested in what he is saying, and that you have come well prepared.

If you want to take notes during the interview, make sure that you do not become so engrossed with your note taking that you lose all "eye contact." There is nothing wrong in holding a note pad, but use it to your advantage. Don't let it become a liability! An applicant who sits there writing all during the interview, as if he were in a classroom lecture, will likely "turn-off" the interviewer.

Another very common beginning for the interviewer to use, would be to simply say, "Tell me about yourself." Now you are "on." This is your cue to show him your stuff. Describe your background in the same basic order as your resume. Begin with your most recent experiences and background. If you begin by telling him how you worked your way through college parking cars, he might lose interest before you get down to the pertinent information.

The advantage of a "face to face" contact is that you can read the employer's face while presenting your background. If you feel you have aroused some special interest at any particular point, then try to draw subtle analogies as to how your experience relates to his needs. Undoubtedly he will interrupt you from time to time with comments or questions. Before you know it, the interview is in full gear. . . .

Occasionally, you are interviewed by one of two extremes:

1.   The first is the guy who just will not respond. He will let you ramble on and on, until you are blue in the face. This is most frustrating, because all the interviewer wants to do is listen. You are sometimes forced to draw him out of his shell by stating, "I have been reading up on your company and your industry . . ." then asking him one of your brilliantly-prepared-in-advance questions.

142

I have had candidates go through a couple hours of the above kind of session, and report back to me that "the interviewer did not say a word." They did all the talking, and left the interview not knowing at all how they did. Sometimes the candidate does very well; but other times, if he is not able to draw out the employer, we get feedback that the candidate talks too much—and he is subsequently turned down.

2.   The second kind of extreme interviewer, is the guy who talks from the moment you enter the room until the time you leave. Do not try too hard to interrupt. Sometimes, in this kind of situation, it is better to just listen. It is amazing, but in the above situation I sometimes receive a report back from the employer that the candidate was excellent. He really liked his credentials and background. The employer will indicate that, "The chemistry was very good."

What he really means is that he himself likes to talk and that the candidate is simply a good listener. There are also occasions, in this kind of situation, where the candidate will be turned down—because he did not assert himself enough. In those cases, he probably should have just interrupted and made a few points. Most interviewers fall somewhere in between. You just have to use empathy, and give your performance when you receive your cue. . . .

When the interview is winding down, the employer may state that he would like to invite you back—for a second set of interviews with some of the other executives. This means that you have passed the first round, and gave a good performance.

Since I am comparing the three major parts of the interview to a Three Act Play, we may as well mention *the patterned stress interview*. This is theatrics at its finest. Fortunately, not too many employers use this interviewing technique. Some industrial psychologists may use it periodically, but fortunately the candidate is a little better prepared for such "games" when they are played by psychologists.

The *patterned stress interview* is simply the interviewer asking a series of questions of the candidate which are aimed to "make his blood boil." They are used, supposedly, to see how much pressure or harassment he can take before he loses his composure.

Patterned stress interviews should only be administered by those who have been specifically trained to do so. When amateurs attempt to conduct these types of interviews they will typically make themselves look silly in the eyes of the candidate. They may even turn-off an otherwise interested candidate. It would not be difficult to lose interest in a company when its representative badgers away at you for an hour with a bunch of irrelevant and irritating questions.

There is nothing wrong with any interviewer asking sensitive questions of a candidate which might give some meaningful clues in evaluating him. In order to find out about a candidate's ambitions, goals, ethics, loyalty, etc., specific questions must be asked. These questions can easily be directed and interpreted in a positive manner.

Follow-Up After Act I

Depending on how and when interviews one and two are scheduled, there should be an opportunity for you to send a follow-up "thank you" note expressing gratitude for the interviewer's interest and time—while also expressing sincere interest in the position discussed. You might also include, in your letter, some brief reasons why your background and experience qualify you for the position. Do not be too lengthy, though. Every employer enjoys having a candidate express interest in his company and specific job opening. It is a sincere form of flattery. Also, if there are other candidates scheduled for interviews after you, a nice thank-you note keeps *your* name before the employer. Several weeks may pass before he completes the interviewing process, so if you were one of the earlier candidates to be considered, *a timely thank-you note is a must.*

One very significant error that candidates make with recruiters and employers is that they are afraid of showing too much interest! Candidates are completely wrong in thinking that it is a sign of

Sample Follow-Up Letter

[Your Letterhead]

January 14, 1979

Mr. John Doe, President
Major Firm
Major Firm Plaza
Chicago, Illinois 60601

Dear Mr. Doe:

   I wanted to drop you a note to express my sincere appreciation for the time you took yesterday to discuss career opportunities with Major Firm Company. I am especially interested in your opening for a Division Controller.

A few reasons why I feel I am qualified for the position are:

1. <u>Experience</u>—Over seven years experience, divided between Public Accounting, and audit management with an industry competitor. I feel my experience provides a good foundation.

2. <u>Education</u>—Possessing both an MBA in Finance, and a B.S. in Accounting should provide me with the academic tools to do a good job. Also, my CPA credentials should lend support to the above.

3. <u>Interest and Desire</u>—Your Division Controllership opening is exactly the kind of position I am looking for. You will note that I began my career in Public Accounting, then moved into industry, developing my audit and management skills as I progressed. I now feel I am ready to become a Division Controller.

Mr. Doe, thanks again for your interest. Hope to hear from you soon.

Sincerely,

[Signed]

Jim Applicant

weakness to express a high level of enthusiasm and interest in a particular job opening. The "hard to get" approach may work in some instances, but it sure does not work when trying to encourage an employer to make you the best offer. If you like what he has, tell him so! Explain why you are qualified, and how you fit what he is looking for. If you want the job . . . ask for it!

Act II

This is the second interview. You will now meet the rest of the "cast", so to speak. Frequently, companies will pass around a prospective employee like an hors d' oeuvre, with all the incumbent management team taking samples. You complete a day like this—and your mind becomes one big blur. If you do not immediately write down the names of the people you met, chances are you will have to call somebody's secretary the next day and ask. Everyone will be wearing their company manners . . . including you.

There are many advantages to talking to a lot of people from the same company before accepting a job offer. You are liable to bump into someone who gives you the inside "dope" on what is really going on. Frequently it will be someone with an axe to grind, but so what! The information you receive, no matter how prejudiced, could be helpful in making your final decision.

Sometimes you will meet several people in the first interview, and then spend most of the second interview with the boss. Each company has their own method and philosophy for hiring.

You may be invited to go to lunch with several employees including a few bosses. These lunches are guaranteed to cause indigestion. Just imagine, you are sitting at a table with six other people who are tearing you apart mentally, while firing pleasant little questions. Meanwhile, you are trying to come across as cool, suave . . . while not choking on your food!

After you have left, all of the people who interviewed you will be

146

asked for their comments and recommendations concerning your hire. The old "fraternity rush game" again.

If your performance came off well during Act II, then you proceed to Act III. If not, then in a matter of days you will receive a "thanks, but no thanks" letter—and the play folds. . . .

While going through Act II of the interviewing process you have to play your role in such a way as not to alienate the other employees. You certainly would not want any of them thinking that you were after their own job—or, using the Three Act Play analogy, you do not want to upstage your reviewers. When going through groups of question-askers, just try to be sincere, intelligent, and polite. Avoid getting cute, or taking any of them into your confidence. Be friendly and charming, but just remember—they are there to evaluate you. Their loyalties are to the company, or at least they should be.

I remember, some years back, I had arranged an interview in Chicago for one of my clients on the West Coast. I had interviewed a very promising electrical engineer who already had his Master of Science degree in Electrical Engineering from the University of Illinois, and had an excellent job with a Chicago electronics firm. We shall refer to him as Bob. The interview was early in the Spring, and I had the client fly Bob out to California for his series of interviews.

When I had originally mentioned that the client was located out on the West Coast, I could sense, even over the phone, that his eyes had lit up. I assumed it was just the typical magical lure of the West Coast climate—especially strong just after suffering a rough Chicago Winter.

As is typical when a candidate visits an employer from a long distance, the first and second interviews were combined into one day. Sometimes the whole "play" or interview process will be combined into one day. A candidate will arrive in the morning—and leave late in the afternoon with a tentative job offer, pending final physical, credit, and reference checks.

Towards the end of what I would call Act II—after the boss had already decided in his own mind that Bob was the right candidate and that he wanted to hire him, Bob was interviewed by a potential peer. Companies often select their "star" employees who are of a similar potential rank as the prospective employee, and arrange to have them talk as equals. This enables the candidate to see some career paths within the company which he can relate to. It is sometimes difficult for a twenty-eight year old design engineer to relate realistically to a sixty year old Vice President of Engineering. Having potential equals interview candidates is much more effective in picking up information. Since the candidate should relate well to whomever the company selects to do the interviewing, valuable comments and feedback will often come out of these meetings.

Bob had already been interviewed by four other individuals, and so far was receiving "rave reviews." Bob ruined his position when the interviewer and he were comparing their education. The interviewer mentioned that he was taking an Educational Leave from the company in the Fall, to complete his PhD in Electrical Engineering. Bob casually mentioned that "I might do the same thing one of these days." After more conversation Bob took the interviewer into his confidence, and indicated that he, too, was scheduled to begin his PhD work at the same West Coast University. At this point it became obvious that Bob had committed a major faux pas. He immediately tried to cover himself by explaining that he had not yet accepted the Doctoral Program opening, and would appreciate the interviewer keeping in confidence the information he had just conveyed. Bob—wrongly—felt he was reasonably secure since the interviewer himself was leaving in the Fall. The interviewer told Bob "not to worry about it," but five minutes after their interview ended, he was explaining to his boss that ". . . all this guy is looking for is someone to pay his moving expenses from Chicago to Los Angeles." The boss immediately cancelled the last two scheduled interviews, and sent Bob home to Chicago. No "free ride" from that company! This was a case of the candidate actually considering a fraudulent act.

As it turned out, the interviewer who was leaving to begin the Doctoral Program checked with the University, and found that Bob had actually signed-up for the Doctoral Program weeks before I ever contacted him. Bob concealed this fact from me, as well as four of five members of the company, but he could not resist responding to the last interviewer's announcement of his own leaving. This is an example of a candidate showing dishonesty and poor judgement—thinking that since the interviewer was of a similar background he would keep quiet and withhold the information. What Bob did not realize, was that three months earlier the interviewer had gone through the proper channels, and received company authorization for leaving to enter the Doctoral Program. It was stupid for Bob to even think that the interviewer might be more loyal to him—a potentially dishonest employee whom he just met—than to the employer with whom he had been happily working for several years. Fortunately, situations like the above rarely happen.

Act III

Once you have passed the first two parts or acts, you are ready for the "Grand Finale" or The Close.

But first . . . if you are married, and the position is in upper management, before you receive an offer you will invariably be requested to attend a session—or as the employer might put it, "a social function"—accompanied by your spouse.

Employers feel that it is most important to evaluate a man's wife as well as the man himself. In some situations this is probably wise, especially at the upper management levels. Unfortunately, I have seen many potential job offers lost because the wife of the boss could not tolerate the wife of the candidate. Of course the candidate is never told, "Your wife just did not measure-up, and could never handle the social requirements which the job demands."

On the other hand, I have seen a charming wife who was just what the boss needed to be convinced that *her* husband was the one who should receive the job offer!

Yes . . . the husbands of women executive candidates are also being appraised before the final offer is made. Again, employers want to know what kind of environment their executive employees are exposed to outside of their working hours. If an employer is considering hiring a female married executive for a position which requires a substantial amount of travel, then the boss rightfully should know if the husband will be supportive of this. Where there is extensive travel involved, the spouse—husband *or* wife—should be interviewed. This is to prevent the employer creating a potential "can of worms."

I am sure that heavy travel on the part of one partner is a major contributor to "problem" marriages. If both partners have careers and travel, there is less chance for one to become disgruntled. If one is left at home, especially if it is the husband, while the other is on the road Monday through Friday—then marital problems could occur. And marital problems frequently bring on-job problems!

Ideally the employer should feel that the spouse is 100 percent behind the potential new executive.

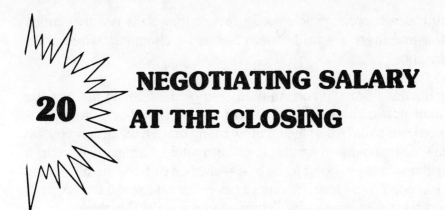

20 NEGOTIATING SALARY AT THE CLOSING

The closing can occur on the first day, or on the third or later interview. Interviews which go beyond three in number soon begin to hit diminishing returns. So, one interview for each part or act . . . or a combination thereof.

We are now ready to talk about the "nitty gritty"—*money*. The employer may have alluded to the subject earlier, but was probably careful not to discuss it in specific terms. Before you make the decision, in your mind, to place an equitable dollar amount on the position, consider the following factors:

How good is the job? If the position is exactly what you have been looking for, then you definitely must weigh that factor accordingly. If the job itself is only slightly better, or equal to, your present one—then money is obviously going to have to come into play much more significantly. In fact, if the job is not that much better and there are no further reasons for changing, why bother changing?

I do not normally recommend changing positions *just for the money* unless the new offer is so fantastic that it will greatly enhance your standard of living. How many times a week can you eat steak? Offers of this magnitude, unfortunately, hardly ever occur. If an offer seems too good to be true—check it out closely. It just may *be too good to be true.* You may have misunderstood the terms of the offer, or there may be "something rotten in Denmark."

Where is the job located? Do you have to pay for any moving expenses? If so, what part? Some items to consider are actual moving expenses, temporary living expenses, closing costs, real estate fees, increased mortgage rates, even new drapes. What portion of the expenses will the employer pick up? These are all substantial expenses which can reduce an otherwise attractive salary increase to a net loss—if a good portion of costs is not absorbed by the company.

Is the new geographical location favorable? Sun Belt companies sometimes pay their employees partly in sunshine. You cannot spend it, but at least it is not taxable—that is, not yet! If the position is located in an undesirable and higher-cost-of-living area, then that all has to be figured out. Some states have very low income taxes, while others may be extremely high! Some states have low real estate taxes, while others are quite substantial. Some states have no personal property taxes, while others are certainly worth thinking about.

If you have children and are concerned about the quality of their education—then you had better carefully evaluate the educational system of the area you are considering moving to. Every state possesses a different attitude towards education. Do not get me wrong, every state *believes* in education. It is just that some states will spend money for a decent educational program, while others seem to have higher priorities.

I have a client located in one of the Deep Southern States.

Unfortunately, the large city where my client is located has such a poor educational system, that my client must add enough money to any offer made to a candidate they want to hire from out of state, to cover the cost of private schools for the children. It is a sad state of affairs when a company has to do this, but those are the facts of life.

I might also mention that this particular State likes to brag about their low taxes. Parents who demand a high quality of education for their children use their tax savings towards private schools!

One of the best sources of help in finding out about a particular city is the local Chamber of Commerce. If they do not have the answers at hand, then they will surely know where to direct you. I have found Chamber of Commerce employees, over the years, to be extremely cooperative in assisting potential newcomers to their community.

The opportunities beyond. Is this going to be your only forseeable opportunity to obtain a substantial pay increase with the new employer? In other words, is this the top job—with no place to move-up with your present background? If there *are* good opportunities beyond this position—either at the corporate or divisional level—then this factor is certainly worth weighing.

Fringe benefits. How do they compare to your present package? Do they have profit sharing, pension plan, major medical, disability, dental, tuition reimbursement, credit union, or any other valuable considerations? Is there a country club membership, or a company car? Does the employer pay bonuses? Does either employer provide a good company cafeteria at reasonable prices? All of these factors, when totaled, will add up to several thousand dollars. There could thus be a several thousand dollar difference between the two fringe packages!

Also, what about vacations and paid holidays? Will you lose or gain on your vacation by switching? This may not seem very important to you, but it just may irk your family to see you go from a present three-week vacation to one week! You must have your family's support. If your family feels they are being short-changed on your move, then you should not change positions unless you absolutely have to!

A job change affects the entire family, so obviously your chances of making a successful move are greatly enhanced when your partner and kids are with you all the way. . . .

Travel and commuting.   Will you be reducing or increasing your percentage of travel and commuting time?

Summing it up

The above factors are all to be considered before and during your salary negotiations. Have you completed your homework in finding out, through some of the previously discussed sources, just what the competitive salary range is for the position? You want to avoid pricing yourself out of the market, but yet you do not want to "low-ball" yourself either.

The employer may begin the final Act by simply stating, "I would like to extend you an offer for [X] amount of dollars, what do you think?" Or, he might indicate that he would like to hire you—and what would *you* consider coming to work for?

Keep in mind that no matter which approach is used to extend an offer—and there are several—the employer wants to pay you the least he can, and you want to receive the most you can get. This is all done in very friendly fashion of course—everyone playing their specific roles.

If you are presently underpaid in your position, and you have indicated your present salary to your prospective employer, do not expect him to make up for what your present employer has failed to do. There is usually only so much of a percentage increase that a company will go to—so, do not blow an otherwise great opportunity by telling the employer that he has to practically double your salary in order to hire you.

If you have checked out the salary range for the position, or even if you were unable to, do not be afraid to ask the interviewer what the complete range of the job is—and also, at where would they

154

like to hire? He may tell you straight out, or give you enough information for you to come up with a good number as to what you are looking for in the way of a starting salary.

Let us assume that all the factors we have discussed were on the positive side. I would then suggest an offer of twenty to twenty-five percent *above* your present *total package*. This is assuming no loss on the actual moving expenses. If there is a loss, then the difference should be picked up in the starting salary.

If all other factors are simply great, and there is no relocation, you might even consider a ten to fifteen percent increase. If everything is just kind of "so-so," then ask for a forty to fifty percent increase. You probably will not get it—but what did you have to lose? You don't think that much of the job in the first place. . . .

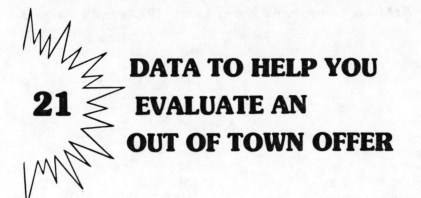

21 DATA TO HELP YOU EVALUATE AN OUT OF TOWN OFFER

Following are some Tables which should help you compare the various Areas and States. You receive a job offer, which on the surface represents a 25% increase over what you are presently earning—but when you analyze all the categories—you may even be losing money by accepting it. On the other hand, if the offer is located in a low cost area; it could be worth substantially more!

There are also a number of other factors which are compared—such as education, police, fire, hospitals, and crime. When an offer is received, one has to evaluate the total spectrum—or putting it another way—"What is the quality of life in the new area?"

Table A: Living Costs for 40 Metro Areas (1977 Family Budget)

Area	Lower Budget	Intermediate Budget	Higher Budget
Northeast			
Boston, Mass.	$11,481	$20,609	$31,199
Buffalo, N.Y.	10,681	18,298	26,818
Hartford, Conn.	10,872	17,796	25,006
Lancaster, Pa.	10,089	16,322	23,273
New York—N. E. New Jersey	11,155	19,972	31,655
Philadelphia, Pa.—N.J.	10,897	17,792	25,933
Pittsburgh, Pa.	10,216	16,516	24,016
Portland, Maine	10,904	17,578	24,796
North Central			
Cedar Rapids, Iowa	$10,170	$16,681	$24,295
Champaign—Urbana, Ill.	10,896	17,223	25,126
Chicago, Ill.—N. W. Ind.	10,789	17,330	25,006
Cincinnati, Ohio—Ky.—Ind.	9,940	16,547	23,289
Cleveland, Ohio	10,476	17,411	25,010
Dayton, Ohio	9,778	15,695	23,185
Detroit, Mich.	10,400	17,427	25,550
Green Bay, Wis.	9,905	16,768	25,114
Indianapolis, Ind.	10,179	16,695	23,806
Kansas City, Mo.—Kans.	10,153	16,486	24,384
Milwaukee, Wis.	10,610	18,230	26,695
Minneapolis—St. Paul, Minn.	10,471	17,813	26,118
St. Louis, Mo.—Ill.	10,043	16,377	23,683
Wichita, Kans.	10,310	15,994	23,168
South			
Atlanta, Ga.	$9,594	$15,483	$22,584
Austin, Tex.	9,286	14,776	21,727
Baltimore, Md.	10,796	17,204	25,308
Baton Rouge, La.	9,572	15,283	22,695
Dallas, Tex.	9,618	15,313	22,500
Durham, N. C.	9,989	16,369	23,514
Houston, Tex.	9,921	15,488	22,421
Nashville, Tenn.	9,413	15,290	22,206
Orlando, Fla.	9,661	14,910	21,832
Washington, D. C.—Md.—Va.	11,084	18,026	26,454
West			
Bakersfield, Calif.	$10,199	$15,686	$22,329
Denver, Colo.	10,188	16,711	24,377
Los Angeles—Long Beach, Calif.	11,134	17,126	25,880
San Diego, Calif.	10,591	16,721	24,908
San Francisco—Oakland, Calif.	11,601	18,519	27,418
Seattle—Everett, Wash.	11,397	17,211	24,487
Honolulu	13,280	20,883	31,987
Anchorage, Alaska	$17,375	$24,019	$34,620

The budgets listed above are not intended to represent a minimum level of adequate income or a subsistence level of living; nor do they represent how families of this type actually do or should spend their money. Rather, they reflect the assumptions made about the manner of living of each of these levels.

Source: Urban Family Budgets—Autumn, 1977 Bureau of Labor Statistics, U.S. Dept. of Labor

Table B: Median home purchase price, by metropolitan area

Metropolitan area	Median home purchase price
Large	
Chicago, IL	$50,900
Houston, TX	46,900
Los Angeles, CA	65,000
New York, NY	48,500
San Francisco, CA	72,000
Washington, DC	68,000
All U.S. metropolitan areas with populations of 1.5 million or more	$49,500
Medium-Sized	
Columbus, OH	$42,000
Hartford, CT	43,025
Peoria, IL	36,000
Portland, OR	35,500
Richmond, VA	42,500
Rochester, NY	42,500
All U.S. metropolitan areas with populations between 250,000 and 1.5 million	$42,900
Small	
Burlington, VT	$37,530
Macon, GA	36,500
Marysville, KS	37,000
Morristown, TN	34,625
Portland, ME	37,500
Yakima, WA	42,000
All U.S. metropolitan areas with populations less than 250,000	$37,000
All of the United States	$44,000

Source: U.S. League of Savings Association. Copyright 1978, United States League of Savings Associations. Used with permission.

Table C: Median expenditures for major elements of monthly housing expenses, by metropolitan areas

Metropolitan Area	Mortgage Payment	Real Estate Tax	Hazard Insurance	Utility Cost	Total Monthly Expenses
Large					
Chicago, IL	$291	$ 64	$ 14	$ 60	$429
Houston, TX	291	48	26	74	439
Los Angeles, CA	403	99	15	50	567
New York, NY	291	111	25	70	497
San Francisco, CA	445	99	20	50	614
Washington, DC	388	85	14	91	578
All U.S. metropolitan areas with populations of 1.5 million or more	$299	$ 70	$ 13	$ 60	$442
Medium-sized					
Columbus, OH	$258	$ 35	$ 10	$ 62	$365
Hartford, CT	240	76	15	70	401
Peoria, IL	247	44	12	70	373
Portland, OR	240	56	10	70	376
Richmond, VA	254	36	12	72	374
Rochester, NY	236	90	13	60	399
All U.S. metropolitan areas with populations between 250,000 and 1.5 million	$264	$ 45	$ 13	$ 60	$382
Small					
Burlington, VT	$229	$ 63	$ 10	$ 52	$354
Macon, GA	243	29	14	70	356
Marysville, KS	249	44	15	60	368
Morristown, TN	236	16	16	75	343
Portland, ME	232	50	14	51	347
Yakima, WA	284	36	13	59	392
All U.S. metropolitan areas with populations less than 250,000	$245	$ 33	$ 13	$ 60	$351
All of the United States	$273	$ 54	$ 13	$ 60	$400

Source: U.S. League of Savings Associations
Copyright 1978, United States League of Savings Associations. Used with permission.

Table D: Per Capita Total Tax Collections of State and Local Governments, 1975-76

1.	Alaska	$1,895.84	26.	Maine	$ 671.92
2.	New York	1,139.94	27.	North Dakota	666.91
3.	California	964.20	28.	Nebraska	657.62
4.	Hawaii	934.68	29.	Kansas	651.27
5.	District of Columbia	924.05	30.	Louisiana	609.84
6.	Massachusetts	902.71	31.	Virginia	609.19
7.	Wyoming	846.56	32.	New Mexico	598.12
8.	Minnesota	822.68	33.	South Dakota	596.32
9.	Nevada	820.32	34.	Utah	592.56
10.	Maryland	814.25	35.	Idaho	590.38
11.	New Jersey	792.83	36.	Indiana	588.14
12.	Wisconsin	790.57	37.	Ohio	585.79
13.	Connecticut	777.84	38.	West Virginia	584.09
14.	Illinois	769.42	39.	Texas	581.29
15.	Delaware	768.30	40.	New Hampshire	571.44
16.	Michigan	749.04	41.	Missouri	570.20
17.	Vermont	742.00	42.	Florida	565.80
18.	Arizona	731.43	43.	Kentucky	548.66
			44.	Georgia	548.65
UNITED STATES		730.52	45.	Oklahoma	529.75
19. ⌈	Colorado	728.00	46.	North Carolina	527.66
⌊	Washington	728.00	47.	Tennessee	493.17
21.	Rhode Island	710.52	48.	South Carolina	489.20
22.	Montana	708.88	49.	Mississippi	486.19
23.	Oregon	703.39	50.	Alabama	455.19
24.	Iowa	700.64	51.	Arkansas	453.74
25.	Pennsylvania	683.91			

Census, *Governmental Finances in 1975-76*, p. 63. Reprinted with permission. National Education Association, Research. *Rankings of the States, 1978*. Washington, D.C.: The Association, 1978, p. 32.

161

Table E: State and Local Tax Collections in 1975-76, As Percent of Personal Income, 1976

1.	Alaska	18.2	26.	Delaware	10.9
2.	New York	16.2	27.	Nebraska	10.8
3.	Massachusetts	13.7	28.	Mississippi	10.7
	Vermont	13.7		New Jersey	10.7
5.	California	13.5		Washington	10.7
6.	Hawaii	13.4		West Virginia	10.7
7.	Minnesota	13.3	32.	Connecticut	10.6
8.	Nevada	12.9		Pennsylvania	10.6
	Wisconsin	12.9	34.	Idaho	10.5
10.	Wyoming	12.7		Illinois	10.5
11.	Arizona	12.6	36.	Kentucky	10.2
12.	Maine	12.5	37.	Kansas	10.1
	Montana	12.5	38.	Georgia	9.9
14.	Maryland	11.8	39.	North Carolina	9.7
15.	South Dakota	11.6	40.	Missouri	9.6
16.	District of Columbia	11.5		Virginia	9.6
17.	North Dakota	11.4	42.	Indiana	9.5
				New Hampshire	9.5
UNITED STATES		11.4		South Carolina	9.5
			45.	Florida	9.4
18.	Colorado	11.3		Texas	9.4
	Louisiana	11.3	47.	Oklahoma	9.3
20.	Iowa	11.2	48.	Arkansas	9.2
	New Mexico	11.2		Tennessee	9.2
	Oregon	11.2	50.	Ohio	9.1
	Rhode Island	11.2	51.	Alabama	8.9
24.	Michigan	11.1			
	Utah	11.1			

Census, *Governmental Finances in 1975–76*, pp. 47–49; and *Survey of Current Business*, August 1977, p. 17.

Reprinted with permission. National Education Association, Research.
Rankings of the States, 1978. Washington D.C.: The Association, 1978, page 32.

Table F: Per Capita Property Tax Revenue of State and Local Governments, 1975-76

1.	Alaska	$1,048.12	26.	Washington	$	235.91
2.	New Jersey	446.48	27.	Indiana		225.88
3.	Massachusetts	430.52	28.	Ohio		223.65
4.	California	415.23	29.	Texas		213.18
5.	New York	411.79	30.	North Dakota		212.28
6.	Connecticut	368.93	31.	District of Columbia		209.50
7.	Wyoming	351.61	32.	Missouri		194.87
8.	Montana	350.25	33.	Florida		191.36
9.	New Hampshire	347.91	34.	Idaho		190.12
10.	Oregon	332.95	35.	Georgia		177.94
11.	Michigan	324.22	36.	Pennsylvania		175.62
12.	Nebraska	318.78	37.	Hawaii		173.52
13.	Vermont	307.88	38.	Virginia		172.63
14.	Maine	297.01	39.	Utah		171.65
15.	Rhode Island	294.14	40.	North Carolina		130.19
16.	Wisconsin	288.60	41.	Delaware		130.12
17.	South Dakota	288.08	42.	Tennessee		129.49
18.	Illinois	283.95	43.	Oklahoma		123.84
19.	Arizona	282.18	44.	South Carolina		115.76
20.	Iowa	277.60	45.	Mississippi		109.59
21.	Kansas	274.06	46.	West Virginia		105.96
22.	Nevada	272.02	47.	Kentucky		104.74
23.	Colorado	271.29	48.	New Mexico		102.51
			49.	Arkansas		101.20
	UNITED STATES	265.54	50.	Louisiana		90.26
			51.	Alabama		57.37
24.	Minnesota	254.20				
25.	Maryland	239.36				

Census, *Governmental Finances in 1975-76*, p. 63.

Reprinted with permission. National Education Association, Research. *Rankings of the States, 1978.* Washington D.C.: The Association, 1978, page 32.

Table G: Local and State Revenue Receipts for Public Schools in 1976-77 as Percent of Personal Income in 1976

1.	Alaska	6.5		New Hampshire	4.9
	Minnesota	6.5		North Dakota	4.9
3.	Montana	6.4		South Dakota	4.9
4.	Utah	6.2		Washington	4.9
	Wyoming	6.2	30.	Louisiana	4.8
6.	Vermont	6.1		North Carolina	4.8
7.	New York	6.0		South Carolina	4.8
8.	Iowa	5.9	33.	Illinois	4.7
	Massachusetts	5.9		Oklahoma	4.7
10.	Wisconsin	5.7		Texas	4.7
11.	Arizona	5.4		Virginia	4.7
	Colorado	5.4	37.	Nebraska	4.6
	Delaware	5.4		Nevada	4.6
	Michigan	5.4		Rhode Island	4.6
15.	Maine	5.3	40.	Kansas	4.4
	New Jersey	5.3		Ohio	4.4
	New Mexico	5.3	42.	Arkansas	4.2
18.	Oregon	5.2		Missouri	4.2
	Pennsylvania	5.2	44.	Alabama	4.1
20.	Maryland	5.1		Hawaii	4.1
21.	Connecticut	5.0		Kentucky	4.1
	Idaho	5.0		Mississippi	4.1
	West Virginia	5.0	48.	Tennessee	4.0
UNITED STATES		5.0	49.	District of Columbia	3.9
				Georgia	3.9
24.	California	4.9	51.	Florida	3.8
	Indiana	4.9			

NEA, *Estimates of School Statistics, 1977–78,* p. 29; and *Survey of Current Business,* August 1977, p. 17.

Reprinted with permission. National Education Association, Research. *Rankings of the States, 1978.* Washington, D.C.: The Association, 1978, page 36.

164

Table H: Per Capita Total Expenditures of State and Local Governments for all Education, 1975-76

1.	Alaska	$973.64	26.	Nebraska	$435.53
2.	Utah	570.03	27.	Massachusetts	434.26
3.	Delaware	566.38	28.	Rhode Island	433.78
4.	Colorado	552.30	29.	Kansas	432.04
5.	Minnesota	549.00	30.	Texas	427.48
6.	Oregon	548.98	31.	Virginia	417.42
7.	Wyoming	540.76	32.	Ohio	416.77
8.	Montana	540.40	33.	Indiana	413.36
9.	California	531.69	34.	Idaho	412.04
10.	Michigan	526.25	35.	North Carolina	410.23
11.	Wisconsin	525.51	36.	Pennsylvania	407.55
12.	Arizona	524.21	37.	Connecticut	400.67
13.	Maryland	516.83	38.	South Carolina	398.40
14.	New York	516.47	39.	New Hampshire	389.87
15.	Washington	515.16	40.	Louisiana	385.08
16.	Vermont	497.47	41.	Oklahoma	381.21
17.	New Mexico	495.82	42.	Maine	378.56
18.	Hawaii	481.80	43.	West Virginia	377.18
19.	Iowa	476.95	44.	Florida	375.65
20.	North Dakota	474.78	45.	Alabama	369.88
21.	District of Columbia	470.65	46.	Kentucky	369.85
22.	Illinois	464.94	47.	Missouri	368.50
23.	Nevada	459.82	48.	Mississippi	363.00
			49.	Georgia	354.73
	UNITED STATES	452.89	50.	Tennessee	352.65
			51.	Arkansas	344.34
24.	South Dakota	451.94			
25.	New Jersey	440.96			

Census, *Governmental Finances in 1975–76*, p. 64.

Reprinted with permission. National Education Association, Research. *Rankings of the States, 1978.* Washington, D.C.: The Association, 1978, page 43.

Table I: Estimated Current Expenditures for Public Elementary and Secondary Schools per Pupil in Average Daily Attenance, 1977-78

1.	Alaska	$3,341	26.	Florida	$1,577
2.	New York	2,527	27.	Nevada	1,571
3.	District of Columbia	2,368	28.	Hawaii	1,568
4.	New Jersey	2,333	29.	Vermont	1,550
5.	Delaware	2,129	30.	North Dakota	1,544
6.	Pennsylvania	2,079	31.	Nebraska	1,526
7.	Illinois	2,058	32.	New Mexico	1,477
	Wisconsin	2,058	33.	Arizona	1,462
9.	Connecticut	2,025	34.	Maine	1,457
10.	Massachusetts	2,014	35.	Oklahoma	1,440
11.	Iowa	2,002	36.	Missouri	1,425
12.	Michigan	1,975	37.	Indiana	1,407
13.	Minnesota	1,962	38.	New Hampshire	1,394
14.	Oregon	1,929	39.	South Dakota	1,385
15.	Montana	1,920	40.	West Virginia	1,374
16.	Wyoming	1,904	41.	Utah	1,363
17.	Washington	1,853	42.	Texas	1,352
18.	Rhode Island	1,817	43.	South Carolina	1,350
19.	Maryland	1,810	44.	North Carolina	1,343
	UNITED STATES	1,742	45.	Tennessee	1,336
			46.	Kentucky	1,298
20.	Colorado	1,708	47.	Georgia	1,290
21.	Kansas	1,698	48.	Alabama	1,281
22.	California	1,674	49.	Arkansas	1,270
23.	Louisiana	1,673	50.	Mississippi	1,220
24.	Virginia	1,603	51.	Idaho	1,193
25.	Ohio	1,581			

NEA, *Estimates of School Statistics, 1977-78*, p. 32.

Reprinted with permission. National Education Association, Research. *Rankings of the States, 1978.* Washington, D.C.: The Association, 1978, page 46.

Table J: Current Expenditures per Public School Pupil in Average Daily Attendance as Percent of National Average, 1977-78

1.	Alaska	191.8	26.	Florida	90.5
2.	New York	145.1	27.	Nevada	90.2
3.	District of Columbia	135.9	28.	Hawaii	90.0
4.	New Jersey	133.9	29.	Vermont	89.0
5.	Delaware	122.2	30.	North Dakota	88.6
6.	Pennsylvania	119.3	31.	Nebraska	87.6
7. [	Illinois	118.1	32.	New Mexico	84.8
	Wisconsin	118.1	33.	Arizona	83.9
9.	Connecticut	116.2	34.	Maine	83.6
10.	Massachusetts	115.6	35.	Oklahoma	82.7
11.	Iowa	114.9	36.	Missouri	81.8
12.	Michigan	113.4	37.	Indiana	80.8
13.	Minnesota	112.6	38.	New Hampshire	80.0
14.	Oregon	110.7	39.	South Dakota	79.5
15.	Montana	110.2	40.	West Virginia	78.9
16.	Wyoming	109.3	41.	Utah	78.2
17.	Washington	106.4	42.	Texas	77.6
18.	Rhode Island	104.3	43.	South Carolina	77.5
19.	Maryland	103.9	44.	North Carolina	77.1
			45.	Tennessee	76.7
UNITED STATES		100.9	46.	Kentucky	74.5
			47.	Georgia	74.1
20.	Colorado	98.0	48.	Alabama	73.5
21.	Kansas	97.5	49.	Arkansas	72.9
22.	California	96.1	50.	Mississippi	70.0
23.	Louisiana	96.0	51.	Idaho	68.5
24.	Virginia	92.0			
25.	Ohio	90.8			

Computed by NEA Research from data in Table H-10.

Reprinted with permission. National Education Association, Research. *Rankings of the States, 1978.* Washington, D.C.: The Association, 1978, page 46.

167

Table K: Per Capita Expenditures of State and Local Governments for Health and Hospitals, 1975-76

1.	New York	$177.77	26.	Texas	$85.46
2.	District of Columbia	171.71	27.	North Carolina	85.44
3.	Georgia	143.80	28.	Iowa	84.96
4.	Nevada	133.93	29.	Ohio	83.74
5.	South Carolina	122.03	30.	Idaho	83.57
6.	Wyoming	119.74	31.	Missouri	83.15
7.	Alabama	117.78	32.	Oklahoma	81.74
8.	Hawaii	117.71	33.	Arizona	80.93
9.	Alaska	110.13	34.	Virginia	72.76
10.	Florida	109.19	35.	Illinois	72.64
11.	California	107.09	36.	Montana	71.48
12.	Mississippi	103.92	37.	Oregon	71.46
13.	Kansas	103.46	38.	Pennsylvania	70.04
14.	Michigan	103.42	39.	Utah	69.94
15.	Tennessee	97.93	40.	West Virginia	68.72
16.	Louisiana	97.54	41.	Vermont	67.96
			42.	Arkansas	66.02
	UNITED STATES	96.37	43.	Washington	65.89
17.	Nebraska	93.02	44.	Delaware	65.86
18.	Minnesota	92.88	45.	New Jersey	65.52
19.	Massachusetts	91.77	46.	Connecticut	62.06
20.	Maryland	90.62	47.	New Hampshire	58.20
21.	Colorado	90.38	48.	South Dakota	54.96
22.	New Mexico	89.26	49.	Kentucky	53.86
23.	Indiana	87.80	50.	Maine	45.51
24.	Rhode Island	87.45	51.	North Dakota	42.02
25.	Wisconsin	86.88			

Census, *Governmental Finances in 1975-76*, p. 65.

Reprinted with permission. National Education Association, Research. *Rankings of the States, 1978*. Washington, D.C.: The Association, 1978, page 40.

Table L: Per Capita Expenditures of State and Local Governments for Police Protection, 1975-76

1.	District of Columbia	$145.42	26.	Missouri	$36.92
2.	Nevada	86.91	27.	Virginia	36.86
3.	Alaska	72.99	28.	Minnesota	34.57
4.	New York	68.44	29.	Georgia	32.69
5.	California	60.74	30.	Texas	32.01
6.	Arizona	59.90	31.	New Hampshire	31.26
7.	New Jersey	55.39	32.	Montana	30.84
8.	Illinois	52.97	33.	North Carolina	30.34
9.	Maryland	51.49	34.	Idaho	30.29
10.	Hawaii	51.23	35.	Nebraska	29.87
11.	Florida	51.16	36.	Iowa	29.40
12.	Massachusetts	50.62	37.	Kentucky	29.23
13.	Michigan	48.67	38.	Tennessee	29.16
14.	Colorado	45.55	39.	Utah	28.89
			40.	Indiana	27.76
UNITED STATES		44.40	41.	Kansas	26.93
15.	Ohio	42.99	42.	South Carolina	26.78
16.	Delaware	42.73	43.	Alabama	26.77
17.	Washington	41.77	44.	Mississippi	26.69
18.	Oregon	41.65	45.	Vermont	26.61
19.	Connecticut	41.60	46.	Oklahoma	26.33
20.	Wyoming	40.62	47.	South Dakota	26.00
21.	Rhode Island	40.38	48.	Maine	25.84
22.	Wisconsin	40.28	49.	North Dakota	23.48
23.	New Mexico	39.47	50.	Arkansas	22.16
24.	Louisiana	39.25	51.	West Virginia	19.58
25.	Pennsylvania	38.62			

Census, *Governmental Finances in 1975-76*, p. 65.

Reprinted with permission. National Education Association, Research. *Rankings of the States, 1978.* Washington, D.C.: The Association, 1978, page 40.

Table M: Per Capita Expenditures of State and Local Governments for Fire Protection, 1975-76

1.	District of Columbia	$42.18		26.	New Mexico	$13.90
2.	Massachusetts	38.10		27.	Louisiana	13.80
3.	Nevada	36.22		28.	Georgia	13.58
4.	Alaska	31.69		29.	Oklahoma	13.43
5.	California	28.13		30.	Indiana	13.08
6.	Rhode Island	28.05		31.	Missouri	12.45
7.	Hawaii	25.86		32.	Kansas	12.43
8.	Oregon	25.84		33.	Minnesota	12.16
9.	New York	25.17		34.	Nebraska	11.43
10.	Connecticut	23.75			Vermont	11.43
11.	Maryland	21.38		36.	Alabama	11.31
12.	New Jersey	21.05		37.	Kentucky	11.07
13.	Washington	19.39			North Carolina	11.07
14.	Ohio	18.91		39.	Iowa	10.98
				40.	Wyoming	10.69
UNITED STATES		18.43		41.	Utah	10.44
				42.	Pennsylvania	10.41
15.	Illinois	18.28		43.	Idaho	10.21
16.	Colorado	18.16		44.	Montana	9.58
17.	Michigan	18.13		45.	Mississippi	8.81
18.	Wisconsin	18.03		46.	Arkansas	8.60
19.	New Hampshire	17.86		47.	North Dakota	8.29
20.	Maine	17.76		48.	West Virginia	8.23
21.	Arizona	16.43		49.	Delaware	7.99
22.	Florida	16.22		50.	South Carolina	7.07
23.	Tennessee	16.18		51.	South Dakota	7.01
24.	Virginia	15.06				
25.	Texas	14.59				

Census, *Governmental Finances in 1975-76*, p. 65.

Reprinted with permission. National Education Association, Research. *Rankings of the States, 1978.* Washington, D.C.: The Association, 1978, page 40.

Table N: Number of Known Major Crimes per 100,000 Population, 1976

1.	Nevada	8,306.1	26.	Georgia	4,809.5
2.	Arizona	7,886.4	27.	Kansas	4,778.4
3.	California	7,234.0	28.	Indiana	4,673.3
4.	Florida	7,016.7	29.	Oklahoma	4,480.9
5.	Colorado	6,782.4	30.	Louisiana	4,361.1
6.	Michigan	6,478.2	31.	Minnesota	4,331.1
7.	Oregon	6,358.8	32.	Idaho	4,270.5
8.	Hawaii	6,322.0	33.	Montana	4,261.9
9.	Delaware	6,264.4	34.	Tennessee	4,258.4
10.	New York	6,225.1	35.	Virginia	4,203.1
11.	Alaska	6,220.7	36.	Maine	4,084.4
12.	New Mexico	6,215.0	37.	Iowa	4,051.4
13.	Massachusetts	5,820.9	38.	Wyoming	3,975.1
14.	Washington	5,794.0	39.	Wisconsin	3,900.7
*15.	District of Columbia	5,688.4	40.	North Carolina	3,881.2
16.	Maryland	5,664.4	41.	Alabama	3,808.3
17.	Rhode Island	5,620.2	42.	New Hampshire	3,611.3
18.	Texas	5,464.4	43.	Nebraska	3,561.9
19.	New Jersey	5,400.5	44.	Arkansas	3,406.7
			45.	Pennsylvania	3,339.9
UNITED STATES		5,266.4	46.	Kentucky	3,296.8
20.	Illinois	5,055.0	47.	Vermont	3,192.2
21.	Missouri	5,034.1	48.	South Dakota	2,640.4
22.	Connecticut	5,004.6	49.	North Dakota	2,514.3
23.	Utah	4,977.8	50.	Mississippi	2,468.3
24.	Ohio	4,948.2	51.	West Virginia	2,319.7
25.	South Carolina	4,906.9			

FBI, *Crime in the United States, 1976*, pp. 38, 40, 42, 81.

*Includes metropolitan area of Washington, D.C.

Reprinted with permission. National Education Association, Research. *Rankings of the States, 1978*. Washington, D.C.: The Association, 1978, page 51.

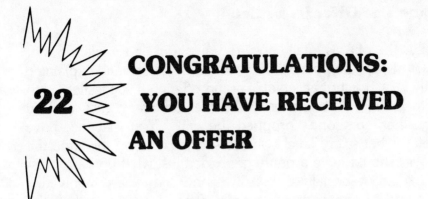

22 CONGRATULATIONS: YOU HAVE RECEIVED AN OFFER

Now what? When you receive a job offer, you can do one of three things:

Accept It On The Spot

Depending on how long the negotiations have taken, how many interviews you have gone through, and how badly you want the job—you may want to *accept on the spot*. This might be recommended when you have completed your other interviews with other companies and have already discussed thoroughly the position with your wife, family, or whomever else you wish to consult. Also, you may wish to consider immediate acceptance when the offer extended is substantially above what you were really aiming for. This rarely happens. . . .

Decline The Offer Immediately

Unless the offer is totally absurd, you should not really do this. There is always the possibility of your coming back and explaining why their offer is not acceptable—and offering a suggestion as to what they might do to interest you. When an offer comes in really poorly, then someone "dropped the ball." You may not have indicated what salary level you are seeking, but by this time the employer should have a pretty good idea just what you are presently earning, especially if there was an intermediary involved. I have heard of employers extending offers of even less than the candidate was earning at the time. Their erroneous logic was that the employer had to take a chance and train the new employee, so therefore the new employee was not worth that much until he proved himself. If you ever receive an offer like that, then you definitely decline. That employer is wasting both his time, and most importantly, your time.

Neither Accept Nor Decline

On most offers you will want to thank them, and ask if you might take a few days to talk it over with your spouse, or whoever, and have an opportunity to reflect on it.

This is especially true if you happen to be still interviewing with other companies. It is always a problem, when scheduling various interviews, about what to do with the offers. Offer 1 comes in, but you know that there is a chance for two more, which might be better. What you might do is this: Depending on how outstanding that first offer is, level with the employer. Tell them that you are most interested in their offer, but have scheduled a couple of other interviews at the same time. Explain that you do not want to accept any position, while you are considering another. They should appreciate your candor and go along with a reasonable request of a week or two to let them know. The only reason that they might not, would be if they have a very strong alternate candidate "waiting in the wings" whom they suspect might not be available in a couple of weeks. It boils down to a calculated risk. If the offer is really great, then you pass by other opportunities. If it is not that outstanding,

174

then you do not want to extend them your answer until you have explored your other opportunities.

You should not accept a job while you are continuing negotiations with other employers. This practice is just plain unethical.

I know of an employer who had gone to considerable time and expense to land a Regional Sales Manager. The Sales Manager had accepted the offered position, but indicated that he could not begin his new position for sixty days. In higher level positions, a sixty day start time is on the long side, but not unreasonable. During the interim, the Executive Vice President, who had made the offer, found out that he was talking to another competitor—even after he had already accepted his offer. How he found out was that his company, of which he was a substantial stockholder, was negotiating confidentially to purchase the rival company, and over dinner the President of the other company casually mentioned that he, too, was trying to hire a Sales Manager. The President went on to describe his prospect's background. The acquiring Executive Vice President thought to himself "that background sounds awfully familiar." Finally, he asked the President who his prospect was . . . and the "bomb" was dropped. At that instant, the acquiring Executive Vice President's face turned a bright red with protruding veins—and he uttered some comments which were, to say the least, not flattering about the character of the Sales Manager.

The Executive Vice President told the President of the smaller firm—"if you make an offer to that guy, and the merger goes through, we will need *two* executives rather than one!" Now, the proposed merger would have the President of the acquired company reporting to the Executive Vice President of the larger one! Needless to say, the offer was rescinded along with some further heated words to the potential Regional Manager. Until the merger went through the Regional Manager was losing sleep trying to figure out just who leaked the news!

The Regional Manager should have indicated when he received his first offer that he was also negotiating with another company and needed more time. If he had been honest, he might have even encouraged a legitimate bidding war between the two potential employers. This sometimes happens when a candidate has more than one offer. Instead, he was not totally honest—and lost both job offers!

Taking The Offer Back To The Boss

Sometimes, the only reason that a candidate will let himself be recruited, or actually go out and seek another position, is because he wants to go back to his boss and say: "Look what I got boss! Another job offer at more money." This technique may work if you are quite valuable, and your company cannot afford to lose you right now! But be careful! I have known executives to pull this stunt, and wind up out on the street. Some employers respond well under this kind of pressure, while others look at it with distaste: Each employer is different, so you had better know who you are dealing with.

I once recruited a labor attorney for a client chemical company. I will refer to him as Howard. Howard did not graduate from one of the more prestigious law schools, so when he started his career five years earlier, he did not command a top starting salary.

My client really took to him, and offered a position with substantially more responsibility and a salary increase of about one third. My client was located in Chicago, as was Howard.

Howard accepted the offer, and when he went to resign his present post I felt he really had no intention of playing both employers against each other. But his employer would not accept his resignation—he indicated that they would beat substantially any offer that he had received—and they did. They offered him a new title, and an increase of forty percent.

The reason that Howard had become so valuable to his present employer was that they could not afford to lose him, at least not at that particular time. Howard was one of the key members of the bargaining team which was getting ready to sit down and negotiate a new contract with the union for the company. His loss at that time would have been most critical.

I warned Howard that his company *had* to offer him what they did. They could not afford to lose him *just then*. Apparently Howard thought he was pretty good, his ego was just too inflated for him to separate "the forest from the trees." He stayed with his employer and received his forty percent raise . . . that is, he received it until they very sadly explained to him nine months later that they were reorganizing the legal department and they just could not afford him anymore. At that time, with his boss just receiving a raise, they were both making the same salary! He had completely destroyed the salary continuity for the department. Such imbalances tend to get resolved one way or another. The company would have had to either bring six other attorneys' salaries up substantially, or pray that they would never find out what Howard was earning, or force him out—as they did!

Very rarely does an executive stay any great length of time with his employer after he has "strong armed" them into a substantial raise. It is a little bit like "blackmail." It may work for a while, but eventually the employer will decide, rightly or wrongly, that you are just not that loyal. You spend too much time getting other job offers. . . .

Frankly, if you have to fight with your employer every time you want a raise, maybe that in itself tells you something. Some employees might not mind going through the turmoil just trying to keep abreast of the cost of living. There are plenty of employers out in the marketplace in all industries who have sophisticated wage and salary programs which are both fair to the employees and bring profitable results to the employer.

23 PUT IT IN WRITING

There are many commitments and obligations in life that should be in writing. Following are four examples, and *why* they should be in writing:

Job Offers

Job offers are usually made verbally—either by telephone or in person—but should definitely be *confirmed in writing*. There are so many facets to the job offer, that it is just not prudent to take a chance of having an honest but significant misunderstanding between employer and employee come up. You want to remove any communication gap.

A written offer should include the job description, salary, bo-

179

nuses if any, fringe benefits, vacation policy, job title, expected starting date, and any other pertinent data that communicates to the recipient just exactly what is being offered.

There is also very good psychological value in having the offer confirmed in writing. If a candidate is considering other offers, or even if he is not, then he has received something tangible before he either quits his job or turns down other opportunities. I have suggested on more than one occasion to my clients, that to expect any executive to give up several years at his present company to join a new one, without first receiving a written offer, is not using good common sense. Yet some employers are surprised when a candidate will not make any commitment until an offer is made in writing.

If an employer does not have faith in the candidate not to simply take the written offer and then play two companies against each other—maybe they are trying to hire the wrong candidate.

Job Acceptance

If the employer should put the job offer in writing; then, likewise, the candidate should *put the acceptance in writing.* First the candidate should accept verbally, either by telephone or in person, and then follow-up with a written acceptance.

Again, you want to eliminate any misunderstanding. Also, if the employer has your acceptance in writing, then there is the added assurance that in all probability you will join the company. . . .

From the employer's standpoint, there is usually less chance for a candidate who has accepted your job offer in writing to go back to his employer and try to use your written job offer as a threat. One of the first questions a boss will ask an employee who comes to him with another job offer and asks, "What ought I to do about it?" is, "Have you accepted it?" If you have, he is less likely to try and negotiate with you to stay.

It not only would be lying to indicate to your boss that you have

[Your Letterhead]

January 1, 1979

Mr. John J. Doe
President, Major Company
999 Elm Street
Anytown, U.S.A.

Dear Mr. Doe:

I am pleased to accept your generous salary offer of [XXX] per year to become your new Plant Manager in Olympia Fields, Illinois.

The additional opportunity to earn an additional thirty percent of my salary as a year end bonus—predicated on profits is greatly appreciated. I find all aspects of your job offer most satisfactory.

I expect to report for work at 8:00 A.M. on Monday, January 15, 1979.

Look forward to a long and mutually beneficial association.

Sincerely,

[Signature]

Jim Applicant

not accepted the offer, when your acceptance has already been received in writing, but just plain stupid! That would be a good way to lose two jobs. . . .

The letter of acceptance should be short, gracious, and to the point. Do not get "wordy." Just tell the boss that you are pleased to accept his generous offer, and let him know when you expect to report for work.

Letter of Resignation

When you do decide to resign from your company and accept that "once-in-a-lifetime opportunity," do not forget to submit your letter of resignation. Many executives fail to do this, but it really is important. These executives erroneously feel that verbally resigning is enough. For one thing, you are placing in your permanent record in the personnel department the exact reason why you left your employer. You would not want, many years later, someone to check you out and hear the clerk in the personnel department innocently state, "We do not know the reason why he left. There is *no* indication on his record."

A letter of resignation should be to the point and very diplomatic. After all, you never want to "burn your bridges." The company you are leaving may buy the new one you are joining! It would not be the first time that an old employer followed an employee to his new employer—via the merger route.

Employment Contracts

The higher the level that one is hired at, the more frequently they are used. Many companies do not use them at all, while others use them at even the lower-middle management levels.

The advantage of an Employment Contract to a prospective employee is that, depending on the terms of the contract, he is protected in an income level for a specified period—vital in the event that his relationship with the employer is severed. This could

182

January 1, 1979

Mr. John A. Doe
President, Major Company
666 Main Street
Anytown, U.S.A.

Dear Mr. Doe:

It is with much regret that I am hereby tendering my resignation as Chief Engineer effective January 30, 1979. As you know, my family and I have wanted to move to Florida for the last several years.

Although I have really enjoyed my ten year association with Major Company, an opportunity to become a partner with a new company being formed down in Sarasota, Florida is a once in a lifetime opportunity for me and my family.

Mr. Doe, I will always have a special warm feeling towards Major Company, its employees, and especially yourself for providing us with a very happy, rewarding, and fulfilling ten years.

Sincerely,

[Signature]

Jim Smith

then be fulfilled in the form of a lump sum settlement, or a continuous salary.

Employment contracts vary all over the map. Some are so simple that they hardly specify more than "while you are employed, you will be payed an agreed upon salary compensation." Others may extend for dozens and dozens of pages, and cover every conceivable aspect of the job—its function, compensation, fringe benefits, unforseen circumstances, severance pay, non-competing clauses, etc.

Employers tend to feel that it is in their own best interest to use employment contracts to assure employee performance, and ensure that the employee will not leave too soon.

I have seen employment contracts cause an employee to literally do nothing for a period of time—just so long as he fulfilled his employment contract of not leaving before a certain date.

The key to a successful employment contract is the spirit with which it is written. It should benefit both employer and employee as well. Some much-sought-after, highly specialized executives will attempt to have their lawyers draft contracts which are almost solely for *their* benefit. This is especially prevalent in professional sports and show business. Some companies will attempt to convince prospective employees to sign contracts which are solely for the benefit of the employer.

Before you ever sign a complex employment contract, I suggest you have it examined by a competent attorney.

24 PHYSICAL EXAMINATION AND CREDIT CHECK

PHYSICAL EXAMINATION

After you receive your offer, but it is still subject to the successful passing of a physical examination; do not resign until you have been notified that you have completely passed your physical exam. Candidates are so elated with receiving a terrific offer, that they frequently cannot resist boosting their egos by telling their bosses just what a terrific job offer they have received.

Unfortunately, offers are sometimes actually rescinded when a candidate flunks his physical. Over the years, I have heard of, and seen, sad situations where serious diseases were actually uncovered by the physician conducting a routine pre-employment physical. Do not be hasty: It usually takes only a couple of days for the results to be completed.

Most companies today have comprehensive health insurance coverage and insurance companies are not too anxious to have companies add new employees to their group plan who have just been discovered to have a major disease. Also, companies are not too happy to waive the insurance in these cases and underwrite the risk themselves.

Another point is that sometimes there could be a "gap" from the time you leave one employer, and the time when you meet the length of employment requirements of the new employer's insurance company. If this is the case, try to extend the coverage of your old employer's health insurance coverage on your own. Many insurance companies will let you pay for your own coverage during this "gap" period. If not, take out a temporary policy with another insurance company just for the "gap" period. It may only be for a couple of months or so, but why take the chance? You never know, and you always want to be protected. . . .

CREDIT CHECKS

Often you will have a credit check made on your background—before an offer is ever extended. If you have any judgements, liens, or disputed bills, you had better straighten them out —you might win the battle, but you could sure lose the war.

Also, if you have any doubts about your credit rating, you might check with your local credit bureau and ask them what your status is. Because of Federal laws requiring credit bureaus to inform inquiring consumers just what their credit status is, they should cooperate fully with you. If they fail to cooperate to your satisfaction, and time is of the essence, then have a friend who uses the credit bureau's services try to find out your status. If you have any blemishes in your credit file, then go to the source and make amends. *A good credit rating is very important.* Many candidates have been turned down for positions because of a poor credit report and nothing else. This is especially true with the higher level or more sensitive positions.

Companies feel, and rightfully so, that if you are going to be in a position to handle the company's affairs, you should have demonstrated that you first know how to handle your own!

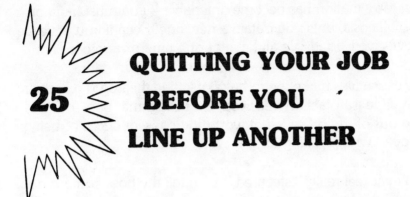

25 QUITTING YOUR JOB BEFORE YOU LINE UP ANOTHER

In 99 percent of the cases, this is bad. Applying for a new position while you are still gainfully employed allows you to deal from a position of strength. Applying for the same position, without already having one, forces you to deal from a position of weakness. Some employers will not even consider a candidate unless he is working . . . as ludicrous as this may be! The erroneous logic behind this thought is "how good can he be? He does not even have a job!" It is sometimes quite difficult to convince an employer that maybe there are some extenuating circumstances as to why a particular candidate is without a job.

I have seen many outstanding executives who were unemployed at one time or another over the years, go on to achieve tremendous success with companies which were willing to take a chance on them. I have also recruited so-called "superstars" for clients, only to have them fall flat on their face in their new assignments.

187

If your job situation has become untenable—you must hang on, at almost all costs, until you obtain a new one! Even if you have to "eat crow", you do it! We all have at one time or another. . . .

Many executives make the mistake of letting their egos rule their brain. A little satisfaction received by telling the boss off and storming out of the office is not worth the consequences of being unemployed while looking for a job.

If you ever feel really "steamed," then tell the boss you are not feeling well, and take a couple of days off. It is much better to do that, than to be out on the street with no job.

Not only is it worse to approach a new employer without already having one, but there are two consequences which will usually occur:

1. *Your reference checks tend to be much more thorough.* Not already having a job is an obvious "red flag"—and all "red flags" are closely scrutinized. I also believe that reference checks have to come through a little stronger and more positive to offset the fact that you are unemployed.

2. *Salary offers tend to be lower.* When the potential employer knows you do not presently have a job, the economic theory of supply and demand operates. Your *demand* is just not as great when you do not already have a job. . . .

A suggestion when you are unemployed and feel you are receiving a "low-ball" offer because of this fact: Counter with, "I really am interested in your offer, but unfortunately it is not competitive with other offers I have recently received within the industry." You may be bluffing, but it is a calculated risk to create a higher demand for your services by potentially creating competition for the supply.

Do not get carried away in this ploy by making up any specific names of other employers who have supposedly made you better job offers. The employer might check with them, and you would end up with no offers! Also, if you really have no other offers and

the prospects are not particularly bright, then accept the offer. A low paying job is substantially better than no job!

I have seen executives who were unemployed for extended periods of time continually pass by job offers because they either did not pay what they felt they were worth, or the job itself was not quite what they thought they were looking for. Meanwhile, they were rapidly eating up their savings. Since we cannot buy groceries with pride, we sometimes should swallow a little of the abundance we all seem to have.

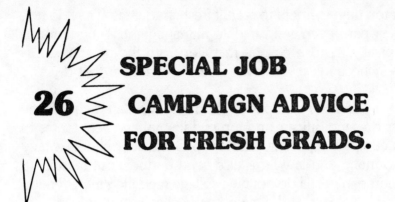

26 SPECIAL JOB CAMPAIGN ADVICE FOR FRESH GRADS.

A substantial part of the subject matter discussed previously could have direct application to graduating students, no matter whether they are at the undergraduate or graduate level. Frequently, when employers come to college and university campuses, the hiring process resembles livestock being judged at a 4-H County Fair. The process is typically hectic, at best. Unless you happen to be a "superstar" in your class, you will probably not command more than the usual twenty to thirty minutes of the interviewer's time. Multiply this times about two dozen per day over a period of several days, and it is no wonder that everyone starts to become "one big blur" to the interviewer. He no doubt will depend on his very valuable twenty to thirty minutes of note taking.

Unfortunately, for the most part, companies do not bother to send their top management to recruit fresh graduates. They do not, for the most part, even send middle management. They unfortunately, typically, send a college recruiter from the personnel department—whose ink on his own diploma is not yet that dry. . . .

There are definitely exceptions to the above statement. Some companies do send officers and top middle management teams to recruit on campus, especially at the top Graduate Schools. Many major accounting and law firms also send partners out recruiting, but most companies still do not give college recruiting the attention it deserves . . . at least, at the majority of colleges and universities.

Companies typically behave like a "swinging pendulum" when it comes to campus recruiting. When the economy slows down a bit, they hate to bother visiting the campuses. A little "flak" from the University Placement Director about their conspicuous absence one year and they will surely be back the next, even if they have no intentions of hiring. Companies cannot afford to alienate the Placement Directors for fear of the upcoming boom years—when they really need to achieve substantial hiring.

Now, my specific suggestion to upcoming graduates is to conduct your own job campaign, while simultaneously scheduling interviews with visiting employers on campus. Use the campus interviews, for the most part, as practice for the interviews you obtain on your own. Use both the resume and the telephone campaign which were previously discussed. Eliminate being exhibited like livestock. You will accomplish this when you select, screen, and approach the companies on your own terms. Believe me, it is a lot better calling up the Engineering Manager of a company and pitching your background over the telephone, than to wait a couple of months for him to send the campus recruiter who will compare you with dozens of other candidates, all of whom he hardly remembers! The best thing that could happen in that instance is that the college recruiter might recommend you to be interviewed further by the Engineering Manager.

By either sending a first class resume accompanied by an appropriate cover letter, or by a telephone call directly to the appropriate department manager, you can capture his undivided attention. Subsequently, you will be evaluated on your own merits—without all the unnecessary college recruiting competition. Quite possibly, you could receive a job offer even before they hit your college campus!

Some companies should be sent resumes, while others you could approach by phone. Use the same criteria for your company selection as was discussed earlier.

There is a lot to be said for the retailers who say, "Avoid the rush, do your shopping early. . . ."

Big Companies or Small?

I am frequently asked where a young graduate ought to begin his or her career. Although there are obvious advantages to both big and small companies, there is no doubt in my mind, that unless a graduate's father owns a small company, he or she should head straight for the big one.

The reason that a large company is the place to begin one's career is primarily the training. Traditionally, in almost every industry, the big companies have the best training programs for career development. What frequently happens is that the fresh graduates will join the big companies, obtain their valuable training, and then get recruited by a smaller company at a substantially higher salary, in a substantially higher position. What will happen is that the smaller companies will pay a premium for the training which has been gained working for the big companies. The small companies cannot economically afford these training programs, so they let the big companies do their training.

Unfortunately, the reverse is *not* usually true. Big companies grow their own management. Very rarely will a big company go to the outside to hire at middle management or higher—unless there are some very special circumstances. And if they did, they would most likely go first to another big company to find their candidate. This is the advantage of having a significant depth of management talent.

If one joins a small company after graduating from college, remains there a few years, and then decides he or she wants to join a big company—it is difficult! To be more precise, *it is difficult to join a big company at middle management or higher.* If you have not stayed with the small company too long, you can always start all over at the bottom of the ladder with some large company. Who wants to do this? So, if you are "sitting on the fence" regarding whether to accept an offer from a big company or small one, go with the big one! You can always change your mind in later years, and some small company will then gladly pay for the prestige and training you have received while working for the big company.

I realize that I am speaking in very general terms, and I am sure that there are many exceptions to what I am advocating, but for the most part this is the pattern which is followed.

Starting Salaries

There are, basically, two essential ingredients for a fresh graduate to command the top starting salary in any given year. The first is to graduate from a "big name" university, and the other is to graduate near the top of your class at that "big name" university.

The lesser the name the school, and the lower your class rank, then traditionally the lower your starting salary.

It is interesting to notice that starting salaries for many categories of college graduates have been increasing at pretty close to ten percent a year for the last few years or so. This means that today's college graduates are starting out not too much less than what the typical graduate of a few years ago is presently earning! The old saying, "if you want to make more money—stay in school" is in many cases literally true.

Is an MBA Worth The Effort?

In general, absolutely *yes*—especially with the larger companies. You not only start out at approximately a fifty percent higher salary,

194

but your rate of growth is also accelerated. In fact, many companies have two "hiring tracks." One for MBAs, where they hopefully will progress rapidly and receive correlating salary increases. Secondly, there is the regular program for B.S. Degrees, where they traditionally "plod" along. They plod along that is, until they wake up and go to a top evening MBA program at the company's expense. Upon completion, they either get promoted, or get recruited away! It is a "caste" system. If you want to rise within the system, then you must take the necessary steps to elevate yourself. You must *make* things happen—they will not happen by simply wishing. . . .

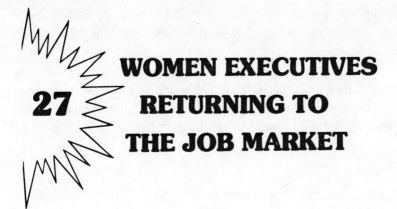

27 WOMEN EXECUTIVES RETURNING TO THE JOB MARKET

One often hears of the woman executive who retires for several years while she has babies and raises her family. Then, when her children are well-grown she returns to the executive job market, only to have a rude awakening. Her executive skills, which have not been used for many years, are rusty. Women frequently become quite frustrated when they first attempt to return to the business arena—and often become disillusioned.

Most of the frustration could be eliminated by simply planning ahead for your return. As an example, if you were a computer programmer several years ago, you will not be trained in what is now being referred to as "the state of the art." Instead of returning to the job market head on—having not even seen a computer for over a decade—go to school first. *Sharpen your skills, and then look for a job.* You must use empathy! An employer wants employees who can step right in and make meaningful contributions. If you are going to be competitive, you must first become prepared. . . .

If you project that you might return to work in a couple of years or so—then the time to prepare yourself is *now*. Start taking some refresher courses at night school. Let your husband watch the kids. . . .

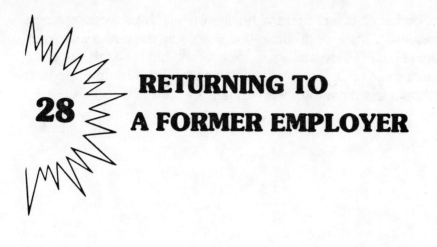

28 RETURNING TO A FORMER EMPLOYER

Over the years, I have seen executives who have left their employers for various reasons—and later on returned. This actually occurs more often than one might expect. In fact, at some companies, the word is, "The best way to get ahead here is to leave and let the company come after you and hire you back."

I would rarely *recommend* returning to a former employer. Unless there is a new top management team running the company since you departed, stay away. Once you leave a company, you should not look back. There had to be a good reason for you to have left in the first place. Frequently, former employees think things have changed at the old company, but usually they have not.

It might be of interest to note that whenever I approach a candidate, on behalf of a client, and he tells me that he is working for his employer for the second time—he invariably expresses interest in leaving again. There are a few exceptions, but it seems the overwhelming majority of these candidates who have returned to their old employers have the "itch" to leave again!

29 PERSISTENCE AND DETERMINATION— A BIT OF PHILOSOPHY

This philosophy applies to literally every aspect of life. Applying it to going to a new job is very apropos. Whether you are trying to land a specific position or conducting an entire job search—*not knowing when to give up* could be a tremendous attribute.

If you send out one hundred resumes and receive no results, then send out three hundred! If three hundred does not work, then send out eight hundred. A very successful insurance salesman once told me that he felt each time he was turned down for a sale, he was just one step closer to obtaining one. With that kind of philosophy, how can you lose?

If you are having difficulty getting past the secretary on the telephone, do not be concerned. Every time you call back, she will feel she knows you a little better; and if you keep on calling, you are bound to get through to the boss. If for no other reason, just so the secretary can get rid of you! The secretary is liable to extend you a "left-handed-compliment" by telling the boss that you just will not quit—you keep calling. *The boss may be looking for someone like this.*

While going through the interview process, you may sense that things are beginning to lag. The progression is at a stand still. You have to get the wheels turning again by calling the boss and diplomatically coaxing him into making a decision. Sometimes you may want to use the counsellor or recruiter for this task. You may want to drop hints that you do have other opportunities that you are considering, but their's is the best, and is your first choice.

Employers sometimes just cannot make decisions regarding who they should hire. After I screen many candidates down to a few for a client, I am sometimes asked "Who would *you* hire?" I try to focus the pluses and minuses of each candidate, but then encourage the employer to make the final decision. I really feel the final selection should be the employer's anyway. A recruiter's role is to screen the candidates down to a final few—but the employer makes the final selection.

Where an employer has difficulty in making a selection decision, I have seen on more than one occasion where an aggressive candidate got the job. You should be quietly aggressive or another way of putting it is: If you were a surgeon, your scalpel should be so sharp and your skill so adept that the patient does not realize he is being operated on—of course he has an anesthetic. Another analogy might be that your persistence should be like those commercials they use to have in the movie theatres. You hardly knew they were there suggesting "delicious, hot buttered popcorn," but before you knew it you had a taste for some and did not know exactly why—habit, you assumed!

PRESS ON

NOTHING IN THE WORLD CAN TAKE THE PLACE OF PERSISTENCE. TALENT WILL NOT; NOTHING IS MORE COMMON THAN UNSUCCESSFUL MEN WITH TALENT. GENIUS WILL NOT; UNREWARDED GENIUS IS ALMOST A PROVERB. EDUCATION ALONE WILL NOT; THE WORLD IS FULL OF EDUCATED DERELICTS. PERSISTENCE AND DETERMINATION ALONE ARE OMNIPOTENT.

INDEX